MORE THAN
MEETS THE EYE

Exploring Nature
and Loss on
the Coast of Maine

MARGIE PATLAK

DownEastBooks

Camden, Maine

Down East Books

Published by Down East Books
An imprint of The Rowman & Littlefield Publishing Group, Inc.
4501 Forbes Boulevard, Suite 200, Lanham, Maryland 20706
www.rowman.com

Distributed by NATIONAL BOOK NETWORK

British Library Cataloguing in Publication Information Available

Library of Congress Cataloging-in-Publication Data Available

Names: Patlak, Margie, 1957- author.
Title: More than meets the eye : exploring nature and loss on the coast of Maine / Margie Patlak.
Description: Camden, Maine : Down East Books, [2021]
Identifiers: LCCN 2020056555 (print) | LCCN 2020056556 (ebook) | ISBN 9781608937530 (paperback) | ISBN 9781608937547 (epub)
Subjects: LCSH: Natural history—Maine. | Seashore ecology—Maine.
Classification: LCC QH81 .P348 2021 (print) | LCC QH81 (ebook) | DDC 508.741/45—dc23
LC record available at https://lccn.loc.gov/2020056555
LC ebook record available at https://lccn.loc.gov/2020056556

♾️™ The paper used in this publication meets the minimum requirements of American National Standard for Information Sciences—Permanence of Paper for Printed Library Materials, ANSI/NISO Z39.48-1992.

Grateful acknowledgment is made to the following publications in which several of these essays first appeared:

The *Ellsworth American* (July 11, 2013) for a shortened version of "Naming Nature," published as "For the Birds."

The *Ellsworth American* (September 5, 2013) for a shortened version of "They Say There Are Moose."

Proximity (March 16, 2016) for a shortened version of "Fog," published as "Out of the Fog."

Persimmon Tree (June 24, 2018) for "Matriarchs and Monarchs."

Hippocampus (September 3, 2018) for "Moment of Zen."

Cold Mountain Review (Fall 2018) for "Shoreline Cleanup."

The Hopper (January 2019) for "Out of Eden."

JuxtaProse (Vol. 20, Summer 2019) for "Rock of Ages."

For my family,
past and present

Contents

PART IV: OUT OF EDEN

PART V: MEANING BEHIND THE MATTER

The question is not what you look at, but what you see.

—Henry David Thoreau

Prologue

The seals swim out to meet my mother.

We are gathered on the weathered gray dock of a rented Maine house, a simple cedar log cabin surrounded by forest, much like many of the cottages we stayed in during summer while my father worked at a nearby biology research lab. Sunlight glints on the water and a cool breeze wafts the distinctive aroma of the rocky coast—a pungent combination of the earthy spiciness of fir, pine, and spruce trees and the fishy smells of seaweed, mussels, and cobbles soaked in brine.

Although my mother grew up in an apartment building in Chicago and lived most of her life tied to the asphalt of various cities, she always loved the summers we spent on the sparsely populated Mount Desert Island in Maine. She took us blueberry picking on the boulder-strewn hill near the lab, frog hunting at the local pond, and clam digging on the bay at low tide. My mom loved looking out at all the beauty by the water—the bay framed by wind-sculpted silhouettes of the trees like those in Japanese paintings, the gossamer fog at sunrise, the rosy hues of the sky reflected in the water as the sun sank.

So we thought it only appropriate to scatter my mother's remains in the Gulf of Maine. Gulls scatter in all directions, crying in protest at our arrival at the dock, and a kingfisher rattles away, flying off his pine perch. On a distant rock outcropping, a cormorant stretches out its large black wings like a cloak. Reflected clouds drift through water dotted with the bobbing buoys of lobster traps.

Overshadowed by the looming mountains behind us, our family huddles on the creaking wooden platform, dwarfed by the backdrop of the expansive blue bay. Both my balding brother and elderly father rest heavily on their canes, while I take a folded piece of paper out of my jeans pocket and quote from a condolence letter Albert Einstein wrote to the widow of a friend. "In quitting this strange world, he has once again preceded me by just a little," I say, wondering if Einstein's notion that time is an endless loop, with no distinctions between past, present, and future, resonates with my gray-bearded brother and father, both of whom have degrees in physics. A pair of loons responds with sonorous laments.

I try to make eye contact with my brother's two grown sons, but they are gazing at the splintered gray boards under their feet. My father is dry-eyed, but my twelve-year-old daughter starts to sniffle. My oldest child, Jake, and my brother's oldest son, Johann, both gangly, slip into kayaks tethered to the dock. After we untie their ropes and give each son a paddle, my brother's wife hands Johann the small cardboard box of ashes and he plies the glassy water, Jake paddling his kayak in parallel.

My husband, Frank, puts his arm around my slumped shoulders, and we watch as my mother's grandsons, boys that had become men while she entered her final years, put away their paddles and together shake out flecks of her bone and ash. How could my mother, whose caramel eyes reflected delight in my every achievement and whose angry outbursts made me cower in my bedroom, be reduced to that small package of dust? While the gray powder falls into the water, it sinks in that I am truly a motherless child. But I wrestle with that biblical notion of ashes to ashes. Surely something remains?

While the last bits of my mother slip into the sea, a few curious seals swim over to see what is falling into their waters. A beautiful swirling dance ensues as their swimming heads engrave the calm water with V's that eventually merge with the kayak's wake. It is entrancing, and though I do not feel my mother is embodied in her ashes, there is something comforting about her being welcomed by these tidal dwellers and returned to Maine and the primordial sea.

Two years later, it is the ash remains of my brother's fifty-five-year-old body that are spread on a mountain in Vermont. He was diagnosed with Lou Gehrig's disease, also called ALS, the week my mom died. Just a few months after we gathered in Maine, my brother became confined to a wheelchair and quickly lost the ability to move most of his body. From the moment my mother was diagnosed with metastatic cancer to the time my father died ten years later, death lapped at the edges of my family like an incoming tide that quickly submerges the small islands it encounters.

Propelled in part by my brother's death and a deepened awareness that life can be short, Frank and I decided to make the most of our own remaining lives. We took the plunge and used proceeds from the sale of Frank's business in Philadelphia to buy a five-acre slice of a northern Maine forest and bay with a cedar, mahogany, and glass Frank-Lloyd-Wrightish house my mother would have loved. We started spending summers there, and after our daughter went off to college, falls as well. Frank always had that business instinct of buying low and selling high and saw having such a house on the coast of Maine as a good investment.

I saw it as an emotional lifesaver.

PART ONE

Call of the Wild

CHAPTER ONE

Telltale Heart

Those who dwell, as scientists or laymen, among the beauties
and mysteries of the earth are never alone or weary of life.

—Rachel Carson, *The Sense of Wonder*

It was still drumming its pulsating rhythm onto my palm, blood
squirting out with each beat.

I was only five when my dad cut the heart out of a dogfish
shark and plopped it into my hand. Most children at that age might
have been horrified at the bloody spectacle filling my palm, and I was
alarmed to some degree. But there was also something puzzling, precious, and thrilling about holding this heart with a life of its own, at
least for the few seconds until it sputtered to a stop.

That day was already unusual because my older brother Joe and I
were spending it with my dad. Normally it was my mom orchestrating
our summers in Maine, taking us blueberry picking or swimming in a
lake so clear it was easy to find and catch tadpoles on its marshy fringe.
But Mom probably wanted a break from us kids, so she suggested Dad
show us his lab, one of several weathered gray cedar shacks edging a
rocky shore. My father worked during the school year as a biomath-
ematician for the National Institutes of Health in Maryland. But in
summer, he joined scientists who journeyed from all over the world to
do research at the Mount Desert Island Biological Laboratory because
of the lab's access to marine experimental animals.

Joe and I ran around looking at all the sea creatures housed there,
scampering from dogfish and skates corralled in pens in the bay, to eels
and urchins in large glass tanks. Seawater piped in from the ocean cir-
culated in the tanks, providing the comforting sound of trickling water.

Then my dad brought us over to the pen that held the dogfish, on which he did his kidney research. With big eyes, I watched him net one of these wild sharks in the pen. As long as I was tall, the slate-colored dogfish thrashed awhile in the net, throwing off a shower of sun-sparkled drops. It was still struggling when we entered my dad's lab shack, and I shrank back from this monster-like creature he had to wrestle onto his lab bench in order to split open its belly with a knife.

In his professorial manner, he pointed out the floppy liver, the long stomach, and the numerous coral-colored gill slits that looked like the undersides of mushroom caps. But what stayed with me most was the heart. Although only the size of a quarter, it loomed large in memory. Like the telltale heart of Edgar Allan Poe, it continued to haunt long after this bloody introduction to biology.

I wanted to know what made it beat.

It must have haunted my brother as well. Years later, after getting a degree in biophysics, Joe went on to research exactly how nerve signals get heart muscle cells to contract. Both of us, like our dad, never lost our childlike curiosity and were compelled to probe what we encountered more deeply and intimately so as to understand how nature worked.

Curious about everything, as a child I lay awake at night trying to understand basic feats of nature. "Why does it rain?" or "How do birds know where they are going when they come back here in the spring?" I asked my dad when he poked his head in my darkened room to see if I was sleeping. With the yellow hall light haloing his head, my father would patiently provide long, detailed answers to each of my questions, solving many of the mysteries that were keeping me up at night.

My mother thought science was boring, except for the science that explained how people interacted and what churned their emotions. A psychology major in college, after my mom had been a housewife for many years, she earned a degree in social work and became a therapist. "So what?" she said when astronauts planted the flag of the United States on the surface of the moon in a televised broadcast that mesmerized millions. "So what?" she said when Joe returned from college and he and my father talked about their research at the dining room table, their hands waving excitedly as they debated the latest theories in physiology. "They're talking science again," she sighed, shaking her head.

Then she pulled me by the hand and said, "Let's go to the living room and read together," assuming my complicity in her disdain. Loving to read and eager for her solitary attention, I followed her, drinking up the camaraderie of women in arms against men of science.

It was my mother who gave me a love of literature, introducing the worlds that could be found between the pages, from glittery and impoverished czarist Russia in *Nicholas and Alexandria*, to Margaret Mead's licentious Samoa. Because of my mother's influence, at a young age I was transported to the misty heaths of *Wuthering Heights* and *Jane Eyre*, and was delighted to enter Frances Hodgson Burnett's secret garden, at one with the main character who nurtured a neglected plot back to its former beauty. Mom was my guide to the written word, the one who edited the school essays and introduced me to poetry. She was so unlike my father, who was a man of numbers, not words. When Dad was a child and forced to write home each week from camp, he repeatedly penned the same exact six words to my grandmother: *Dear Mom, I'm good. Love, Cliff.*

Neither parent expected me to pursue science. This is not surprising given that it was the sixties, a time when most women did not venture into professional careers other than teaching or nursing. When the second wave of feminism crested in the 1970s, my mother went along with the tug of that tide, urging me to mark law as my intended major when applying for colleges. I complied, unaware of a scientific mind that lay hidden behind a heavy curtain of both societal and familial expectations. But after arriving at the University of Wisconsin and flipping through the pages of a thick book listing all its course offerings, I was drawn to classes that could answer my questions. Needing to know what formed the stars and galaxies, I signed up for astronomy. Needing to know what made the houseplants lining the dorm windowsill thrive, I signed up for horticulture. Needing to know how the birds navigated their migrations, I signed up for ornithology. All the courses I wanted to take were science courses except for a course on English literature, warm memories of reading together with my mom on the couch dictating that choice.

You'd think certain episodes in my childhood would have deterred me from science. Like the time my parents' friend, who researched spinal cord disorders, kiddingly asked if he could use our dachshund Moxie for one of his experiments. Being only six years old at the time and not realizing he was joking, I was horrified and always hid Moxie in my room whenever he came to visit. Or the time we received a letter notifying us that our pet guinea pig had been accidentally sacrificed. My father asked his lab in Maryland to take care of the animal over the summer when we were in Maine, but somehow the lab tech confused our black-and-white spotted Scruffy with the experimental animals and it became a martyr for scientific explorations.

Neither of these episodes stemmed my urge to explore deeper. Like a spelunker encountering the sparkling stalactites and stalagmites of a calcareous castle buried deep underground, I was amazed to discover the intricacy and beauty of the orderly onion skin cells seen under the microscope, surprised by how many galaxies there are and the life cycles of stars, and fascinated by the habits of birds. The more I learned, the more flabbergasted I was by the natural world. I was especially enamored of my botany class, having signed up for it after taking a horticulture class that taught me how to help my plants grow, but not the mechanics of how they carried out the fantastic feat all on their own.

I decided to major in botany, eager to learn what propels water all the way from roots deep underground into the leaves of towering trees hundreds of feet tall, and to delve into the chemical wizardry that enables a chlorophyll-laden cell to grab sunlight and turn it into food. I explored this new territory of plants as if I were the naturalist Meriwether Lewis undertaking that famed expedition west with William Clark, astonished by all that I was uncovering.

After completing my master's degree in environmental studies, I decided to become a science writer, so rather than being limited to answering just a handful of questions with my own narrow line of investigation, I could delve into all areas of nature that fascinated me. Applying my mother's honing of my reading and writing skills to science writing, I used this profession to try to answer questions that kept popping up; questions that still kept me up at night, rummaging through research articles, books, and the internet; questions that my dad could no longer answer.

My father's once-dark hair has thinned on top late in his life and, without my mother to remind him to cut it, grows silver, long, and with a frizzy fullness on the sides like Einstein's. His white beard also is full and fluffs out his jawline.

Fifty years later, he and I return to the lab where I held the magnificent beating dogfish heart in my hand. Many of the shacks have been rebuilt, expanded, and updated to accommodate new technology needed for the genetic and other fine-tuned experiments. Such explorations on the molecular scale comprise the bulk of research that scientists conduct there now. This research uncovered a molecule found in the dogfish that fosters repair and regeneration of heart tissue and may lead to new drugs for heart disease. My dad could use such treatments for his own deteriorating heart. He slowly plods along, leaning heavily on his cane. He stoops where he once stood tall, totters where he once strode.

As we inch our way from one lab building to another, my father bemoans the direction biomedical research has taken; its scalpels of discovery have become miniaturized, automated, and computerized to the point of intangibility. For him, there is little drama in the dissection or excitement in the exploration now that most of the answers researchers seek today can be found by plying the genes in a single drop of an animal's blood.

But the questions the scientists are trying to answer are just as compelling: What underlies a salamander's ability to regenerate a lost limb? What enables sea urchins to live for a century? How do fish frolicking in both fresh and salt water adjust to different salt levels? There is still that endless quest to understand Mother Nature; the more we uncover, the deeper we have to dig to find the underlying mechanisms, to find out what makes her tick.

To get to the heart of the matter.

And yet such scientific explorations can never answer the ultimate questions. *Where did she come from?* I thought when my daughter's round, ruddy face poked out of her white swaddling blanket, and I felt her tiny fluttering heartbeat close to mine. Less than a year later when my father-in-law died and my mother-in-law dropped his remaining shoes into the hospital pail with a loud thud, I was similarly stunned and asked myself, *Where did he go?* Then once my mother died, a new question surfaced: *What remains?* These are questions I need to ponder while watching seals swim through water that once supported my brother's sailboat and now harbors my mother's ashes.

The meaning is there—I just have to find it.

CHAPTER TWO

Call of the Wild

> While we readily accept that a healthy seed can't grow into a plant without the right soil, light, and water, and that a feral dog won't behave like a pet, we resist recognizing the importance of environment in our own lives.
>
> —Winifred Gallagher, *The Power of Place*

Compelled to break out of the monotonous confines of square lawns and sidewalks in the Philadelphia suburb where I live, I walk in a nearby stand of beech, poplar, and aspen trees fed by a network of small creeks and draped with vines. The dense greenery is comforting but constrained by a border of identical neocolonial houses whose rectangular windowpanes overlook the ravine. It is spring and I hope to find one of those surprises in nature that take your breath away—toads that hop out in front of you like those on the paths in Maine forests or the pendulous pouch of a lady's slipper orchid emerging from the leaf litter. Instead there is the suffocating dull sameness of English and poison ivy creeping over the forest floor and smothering the tree trunks, with no sudden flutter of a surprised grouse or a carpet of pink trilliums to break up the endless green. Even sounds lack diversity, dominated by screeching blue jays and cawing crows. There is no nasal honking of nuthatches or high-pitched trilling of wood warblers, no rhythmic crunching of leaves due to some mysterious creature leaping away. This suburban oasis will never be wide and wild enough and makes me feel like an animal caged within a zoo's natural enclosure that provides a false sense of freedom.

I need to escape.

Although I could do my freelance writing from anywhere, I resigned myself to raising our family in this suburb, where there were better schools for our children, better work opportunities for Frank. But there was a part of me that always longed to be in the wilder environment I experienced in Maine as a child. I wanted to be amazed by a chorus of coyotes at sunset, spy a pair of fox kits tumble their way out of the forest, or be mesmerized by fog linearly lumbering its way down the bay at dawn, erasing all boundaries and imparting a sense of the unknown in its wake.

In his book *The Moth Snowstorm: Nature and Joy*, British environmental journalist Michael McCarthy notes the pure joy a natural environment gives us. This joy stems in part from wonder at the unexpected and the mysterious, such as the awe induced by spotting a whale's tail slap the water, which can put us in touch with an entire universe underneath we have yet to explore. "We are astonished to be in a world which can contain such a phenomenon, and somehow the astonishment then reaches out beyond the sense of our place in the world, and to the fact that we exist at all," he wrote. Such experiences in nature can disrupt our normal frame of reference and make us more curious about what is around us, restore a childlike sense of wonder that draws us out of ourselves to explore a bigger realm, just as the low tide on the Maine shore prompts snails to emerge from their shells and venture from one rock to another. "It gives you a different perspective on the world when you stand in a place that is wild and you realize you are one species of many," a park volunteer said in the video *In Celebration of Open Space* by Tate Yoder. Another woman added, "Large open spaces remind us how small we are."

Others in the video talked about how wild open spaces can be energizing and healing, how they are "the natural medicine that no one has explored enough," with one park volunteer noting, "We energize our bodies by eating and sleeping, but we never energize our souls until we set them free in open space." Studies are beginning to document the benefits of experiencing nature on psychological well-being, showing that time spent in natural environments can reduce stress hormones and negative ruminations, while boosting happiness and providing a sense of meaning and purpose in life.

Some experts claim being in nature also gives us peace because the natural environments from which we evolved have shaped our psyches.

So we feel more at home within them than surrounded by the recent inventions of cities and suburbs. We are hardwired to expect certain things from landscapes, and modern artificial landscapes violate those expectations. The natural world is "where we became what we are, where we learned to feel and to react. There is an ancient bond [with it] surviving deep within us which makes it not a luxury . . . but part of our essence," McCarthy asserts.

I want to renew that ancient bond.

"Look Mom, it's eating it!" twelve-year-old Jake says, pointing at the bald eagle on a lofty spruce perch, tearing a fish apart in its curved beak. We spot the eagle while kayaking in the bay by the house we are renting in Maine. There are unobstructed views in all directions on the water, and the rhythmic sounds of our paddles splashing are interrupted only by the occasional chortle of a loon or buzz of a tern. The bay is so calm and reflective it feels like we are paddling through the sky, our kayaks kissing the clouds.

Deeply breathing in scents of sea and seaweed, I have finally slowed down the dizzy pace of life enough to notice and appreciate our surroundings.

For much of my adult years, I scurried from one task to another without deliberation, like a rat on a mission. My mission was to make a living and raise a family. This meant most days were spent indoors tied to a desk or tending to children while trying to meet one deadline after another. Once an editor from a magazine called while I was cooking dinner and simultaneously trying to prevent my highly active two-year-old from killing himself. "Do you think you can get that article to me by next week?" she asked. "Sure, no problem," I said, while extending the telephone cord so I could grab Jake before he ventured too close to the stove. After hanging up, I was both thrilled that she wanted my article and terrified that I wouldn't have time to write it.

When you are growing a family and a career at the same time, you live moment to moment, life fast-forwarding with no stop-action. There were always stories waiting to be written, children waiting to be fed, a house waiting to be cleaned. So I operated reflexively rather than reflectively. But while vacationing in Maine, there's time to hover above my life like a kingfisher above the water before it nabs a fish, noticing and savoring everything dived into.

Spying kingfishers and eagles are just some of many treats experienced in Maine that week. A few days later while I'm swimming breaststroke in the bay, ecstatic by not being confined to a lap lane, the sinuous black head and neck of a cormorant pops out of the water only a few feet away. This encounter surprises both of us, lasting only moments before the bird uses its wings to flap it into the air, splashing the water in the process. The crowning moment of the vacation is when we wake up to glinting on the blueberry bushes of dozens of spiderwebs catching the glitter of dewdrops, astonished and grateful that such simple, commonplace, and natural elements of water and light had transformed the ordinary into the extraordinary. On our final night, while watching the disappearing light of the sun pink and pearl the undersides of fluffy clouds reflected in the water, I ask Frank, "If you knew this was the last sunset you would ever see, do you think you would enjoy it more?"

"I suppose so," he answers. "Wouldn't you?"

"No, because I'm really enjoying it right now," I say and take a deep breath, releasing it as a sigh. In those busy middle years, my family could spend only one week each summer in the lobster state.

It was never enough.

At the end of our vacation, when finally relaxed enough to fully smell the pine and balsam scents and reflect on the course my life was taking, I would have the same realization: I craved the daily connection to nature I was receiving only annually. I needed the perspective gained by hiking to the top of a mountain and seeing all signs of human habitation disappear, by merging my kayak-encased body with that of the capacious bay, or by lying on the ground on a clear night, counting one shooting star after another against the glowing backdrop of the Milky Way. I was suffocating in the suburbs, desperate for deep breaths and the sense that there was a bigger, wilder world out there to explore.

Summers spent in Maine as a child must have shaped me in certain ways. I expected to see a fox flaming out of the forest, not a dog on a leash leading back to its human counterpart. I wanted to pick wild blueberries while hiking up a mountain, not a carton of fruit plucked from a store aisle. I longed for a shore filled with rocks and rockweed, not a sandy beach lined with people sunbathing on towels, covering the entire terrain like a deck of cards splayed out in the game Concentration. When we came home from our vacations in Maine, mental and physical muscles stretched by all the outdoor activities soon atrophied, the awe buried under the mounds of laundry, mail, and other piles of responsibilities awaiting our return. It was hard to fit into the contours of the suburbs, and a sort of dormancy ensued.

Dormancy is a defensive strategy plants often use when they encounter unfavorable growing conditions. Sometimes it is for only a season—a cold winter for a tree, a dry summer for a moss—during which growth is put on pause mode until a more welcoming environment returns. Seeds have an amazing capacity for dormancy; Israeli scientists were recently able to coax dates stored at Masada, site of the famous rebellion of the Hebrews against the Romans, to sprout and grow into palm trees, even though the fruits were dried nearly two thousand years ago. All they needed was the proper growing conditions. But plants can also be remarkably finicky about what those proper conditions are—the spores of one species of moss will sprout only on deer droppings left in a bog, whereas another favors coyote scat in a forest; a sedge will edge a marsh, but not live in its deepest and wettest center, where cattails thrive.

While conducting my master's degree research on a wetland in southwestern Wisconsin, I learned firsthand how various factors in an environment dramatically determine what will flourish there and how dormancy will ensue if those conditions aren't met. Friends called me the Marsh Maiden then because I was always immersed in the muck of my muse—a small circular patch of reeds, sedges, cattails, and bulrushes that grew out of a base of glistening water. I was determined to return this pothole marsh to its natural state so it could once more support the whooping cranes that flew past it each year. Due to hunting, pesticides, and habitat loss, there were fewer than a hundred of these striking stork-like birds left in the wild in the early 1980s, when I began my research, and the potholes that dotted the Midwest landscape were their lifesavers. Like turnpike rest stops, the marshes provided food for the birds as they flew from their nesting grounds in Canada and the northern regions of the Midwest to their wintering grounds in the southwestern United States, Mexico, and Florida.

Farmers had drained or filled in many of these marshes with soil and planted them with reed canary grass or other exotic plants, whose seeds are as unpalatable to native birds as dog food is to us. Such drainage, fill, and farming had nearly obliterated pothole marshes in the Midwest and contributed to almost eliminating the whooping crane, large birds as tall as a person and feathered white as snow except for a cap of scarlet feathers and long ebony legs.

These birds have an especially extensive lineage, which made their possible extinction all the more tragic. As Aldo Leopold, the father of the wildlife conservation movement, wrote in *Sand County Almanac*, when we hear the call of a crane, "We hear no mere bird. We hear the trumpet in the orchestra of evolution. He is the symbol of our untamable past, of that incredible sweep of millennia which underlies and conditions the daily affairs of birds and men."

The whooping crane's loud mating call Leopold referred to sounds more like it emerges from an elephant than a bird. To ensure that this unusual animal aria continued to stun future generations and make them realize there is more to this world than they could have possibly imagined, I was driven to help save these birds in the wild.

The pothole marsh I was trying to restore had been invaded by reed canary grass, which, like an unruly cancer, had rudely obliterated much of the variety of the plants living there. Because of the incredible ability of plant seeds to endure until the time is right to sprout, removing those invasive plants should let the original marsh plants return. That return hinged, however, on whether the original water conditions the plants depended on were still present.

To reveal those water conditions, I enlisted the help of Charley Bradley, a retired geologist, who helped me dig several holes in the muck of the marsh in which we placed pipes we could use to measure water levels. Tall and balding and Aldo Leopold's son-in-law, Charley was in his seventies but fit and as eager to uncover the water-flow dynamics in my marsh as I was. We traipsed across the meadow lugging several PVC pipes and shovels, the hot sun inescapable with no shade trees in sight, locusts rattling in protest. By the time we got to the marsh, we were drenched with sweat and trailed by a swarm of mosquitos. Fortunately, a dazzling herd of dragonflies came to our rescue, darting around the marsh, nabbing the insects in a brilliant display of iridescence.

I had only a day to fit this task between working nearly full time at another job and taking classes. This hectic lifestyle offered little opportunity for rest and reflection, so I envied Charley's empty schedule. "It must be nice to have the time to do whatever you want now," I said to him, while shoveling.

Charley sighed and, towering over me with both height and experience, looked down and said, "You'd think so. But now that I've got all this time on my hands, what do I do with it? I spend it regretting all the things I should've done but didn't 'cause I was too busy. I never got the chance to reflect on whether I was taking the right path." I dropped my shovel, surprised by his frank and unexpected response.

Charley's comment continued to jab whenever I reluctantly returned from our Maine vacations. *Was I on the right path, living in the right place?* But ultimately it was Joe's life and death that sent me back to a wilder environment. As a freshly minted PhD, Joe worked in the lab of a researcher who pioneered a technique enabling scientists to eavesdrop on the electrical chatter of a single nerve cell. Joe could have sailed on the tailwinds of this Nobel Prize–winning scientist into any choice academic position. Instead he chose to sail on Lake Champlain in Vermont, where he took a more humble position at the university there. This enabled him to have the lifestyle he wanted, hiking, boating, and raising his two boys. "I have no regrets," he told me while pondering his imminent death. "No regrets."

I wanted to be saying the same thing when lying on my deathbed.

Once Joe died, I responded to the siren song of the sea, to the subconscious beckoning of the deep forest and overshadowing mountains, to that call of the wild as jolting as the bugling of a crane. I returned to Maine—this time to find a home.

PART TWO

Sharpening the Senses

Touching the edge of the unknown sharpens the senses.

—Rebecca Solnit, *A Field Guide to Getting Lost*

CHAPTER THREE

The Nose Knows

Smells are surer than sights and sounds
To make your heart strings crack.

—Rudyard Kipling, *Lichtenberg*

They just don't smell right.

There is too much birch and beech, not enough balsam. Too much sea-spray scent, not enough bay mud. The real estate agent takes us to all kinds of oceanfront properties, including those with surf crashing on granite rocks below or with the clamor of cobbles tumbled by waves. Although they are beautiful houses with post and beam construction and large windows that look out at the spectacular scenery you would expect from Down East Maine, I am not drawn to any of them. They don't move me.

Nothing resonates.

After rejecting yet another shore house surrounded by forest, I realize I am not looking for a house but a home—a place filled with childhood memories in which my brother and mother could come alive again. Wanting to open a door closed by their deaths years ago, I know the best way to do that would be to follow my nose.

Scents and tastes can transport you. What Proust knew so well, when a bite of sponge cake suddenly time-travelled him back to teas spent with his aunt, is that smell and taste can trigger intense memories. Scientists suspect this is so because these sensations' nerve signals travel first to the memory-containing regions of the brain before passing through and being edited by the region that makes us consciously aware of what we are experiencing. The direct highway that connects what you smell and taste to what you remember makes memories triggered by them often indelible. Smells and tastes powerfully and subliminally affect us.

That's why the sweet-sour taste of wild blueberries takes me far back in time and brings to the fore my mother, who often took me blueberry picking while summering in Maine. Blueberries grow on rocky stretches of land where the soil is thin and the sun strong. Unlike store-bought blueberries, Maine wild blueberries burst with tangy flavor. But these berries are *so much smaller*. It takes seemingly endless hours for a small child to fill a pail with them. My mother and I would spend entire afternoons bending over one blueberry bush after another. I would follow my mom's red bandanna kerchief, a beacon in the blueberry field, as it rose and fell in the boulder-laden landscape like a scarlet float bobbing in the waves.

In my case, the initial ping of the blueberries hitting the tin bottom of the pail rarely was followed by the dull thud of blueberries landing on their brethren below because most of the sun-warmed berries I collected made a tasty entry into my mouth. But my mother never minded. And I never minded the hours spent picking blueberries because I knew they would result in a delicious pie I would help my mom make. Minutes after being placed in the oven, the smell of berries and sugar melting and merging inside the buttery skin would seep out of the kitchen and waft into every room of our cottage, making the wait for the pie to brown unbearable for my small stomach already grumbling in anticipation. "Is it done yet?" I would ask my mom every five minutes until finally she put a steaming slice on a plate before me, its sweet ooze coloring my mouth purple after the first bite and staining an indelible memory in my mind.

Unlike the aroma emitted by a baking pie, many smells in nature swirl underneath our noses undetected because we rely less on our sense of smell than the bulk of the animal kingdom, which depends on scents for life-sustaining purposes such as to find food or a mate. Once when hiking up a mountain, I stopped to sit on a ledge and admire the plunging view while quenching my thirst with a peach. Within minutes of biting into this especially juicy piece of fruit, I looked down and noticed a thin black line extending from the salmon-colored granite rock on which I was sitting to a nearby mini mountain of sand a few feet away. This line was comprised of dozens of ants relentlessly following each other to the peach juice that had dribbled onto the ground. I could understand why ants would seek out the sweet drops, but why such a thin line? Wouldn't the ants that surrounded me be drawn from all directions like iron filings drawn to a magnet?

Years later I found an answer while doing research for an article on pheromones: the straight line was made by ants following a scent trail laid down by the first one to discover the peach juice. As it returned to its home base, the scent tracks made by this pioneering forager, like repetitive roadside billboards, told the other ants in the mound where to find food. Although I couldn't sense it, the narrow olfactory pathway followed by these ants was as brilliant to them as the yellow lines on highways are to drivers.

Similarly, as pine bark beetles tunnel through the outside rind of pine trees, they exude a scent that draws larger crowds of their kind to overwhelm the tree's sticky resinous defenses. This beetle scent is composed of three different chemicals and only the right proportion of all three will attract the beetles, just as only the right proportion of balsam, pine, fir, and mudflat scents would draw me back to Maine. Scents guide salmon for thousands of miles on their journey back to where they were born. A newt can smell its way home from as far as eight miles away. The nose knows.

Scents are particularly powerful among the miniscule, which are difficult to spot visually and must rely on other ways of announcing their presence. Insects often give off amazingly strong smells to others of their kind, despite the minute amounts of scent exuded. Such entrancing aromas can attract potential mates from great distances. One researcher documented a single caged female pine sawfly that drew more than eleven thousand male admirers from the field in less than five days using her seductive scent, which the human nose lacks the sensitivity to detect.

Alas for most insects, love is truly blind. Male moths have been observed trying to mate with plastic tubes containing the sex scents for their species, and one scientist who worked with the gypsy moth sex scent reported that he persistently drew male gypsy moths to him after inadvertently getting the substance on his clothing. I love the image of this man being trailed by a floating parade of lusty moths.

We are not as discerning as insects, perhaps, but we still retain the ability to detect more than a trillion scents, including many odors we don't consciously realize we are smelling. Some of these smells enable us to recognize our kin. Dr. Johan Lundström at Monell Chemical Senses Center in Philadelphia had women smell the body odors embedded in armpit pads of shirts worn by their sisters or their close female friends and then asked them to distinguish the two. Although most expressed frustration at this seemingly impossible task, they "guessed" correctly nearly eight out of nine tries. "It's really amazing," he told me. "People are better at picking out kin odors than at picking out a stronger odor, like the scent of an apple."

Clothing often retains the unique scent of a person long after he departs. The night my father-in-law Erv died, after days spent at the hospital, we leave the continual bleeping and bustling and return to my mother-in-law Eileen's apartment. It is intensely quiet, which normally would be rewarding after the clamor of the hospital, but the quiet is accompanied by a profound absence given that Erv is not there to greet us with his warm smile and stress-relieving humor. Erv would do anything for a laugh, including slapstick routines of walking into walls or bringing a spoon up to his eye instead of his mouth. He told his grandchildren that hair would sprout on his bald head wherever they kissed it. A man with big lips, eyebrows, and nose and an expressive face that melted into the contours of any emotion, he drew the attention of a talent agent who put Erv to work acting in commercials after he retired from his family's scrap metal recycling business.

Eileen, in contrast, keeps more inside of her. She is a practical person who takes pride in having an orderly home, in which the socks are all matched and lined up neatly in the drawer and the dishes never tarry long in the dish drainer before being wiped and put away. Eileen likes to keep busy and responds to the long vigil in the hospital—the somber passage of Erv from loved one to corpse, the loss of her husband of nearly fifty years and soul mate for life—by doing the laundry. She starts by pulling all of my father-in-law's shirts off their hangers and throwing them into a laundry basket. "What are you *doing*, Mom?" my sister-in-law asks her, almost panic stricken. "I'm washing Dad's shirts," she says.

"*Don't*—please don't," my sister-in-law pleads, her voice broken. "They still smell like Daddy."

Even though her scent still lingered in them, I didn't hesitate to get rid of my mother's clothes after she died because they reminded me that she wasn't there. Those things my mother and brother left behind triggered my grief—glasses that once marked their faces lying abandoned on bedside tables, my mother's voice on the answering machine, my brother's sweater draped over a chair. I wanted those remnants to vanish so I could adjust to a world without a mother and brother. *Life is for the living*, my logical mind insisted, and I gallantly charged forward, trying not to think about them. But then a letter my mother wrote would fall out of a book, a picture my brother took would slip from beneath shelf paper lining a dresser drawer, or I would see one of them in a dream, and a shard of memory would suddenly pierce my mental armor and remind me that though they were gone, they hadn't truly disappeared and instead were firmly embedded in my memory, causing me to still miss them. I needed to learn the "art of not forgetting but letting go," as the essayist Rebecca Solnit wrote in *A Field Guide to Getting Lost*, because to forget the past is to lose "memory of an absent richness and a set of clues to navigate the present by."

There is something seductive about smells that goes beyond any sexual or kin recognition effects they might have. At a lecture on how to identify and collect edible mushrooms, it is hard to pay attention to the vital distinguishing details between poisonous and edible mushrooms because of preparations for the dinner to follow the lecture. Enticing aromas from the nearby kitchen sneak into the lecture room and eddy under our noses, disturbing concentration.

Appropriately, the dinner features chanterelle mushrooms as the main course, served in a cream sauce that covers a bed of rice dotted with fresh tarragon. I had already tasted chanterelles because shortly after we moved into our Maine house, my neighbor Mary showed me some on my own property. From then on, whenever biking I had my eye out for these bright orange mushrooms, which often grow alongside the road. Chanterelles are beautiful to behold with their undulated edges underlined by numerous crinkled pleats; their intricate, coral-like forms make them seem like they belong under the sea and not on the forest floor.

But what makes chanterelles especially enticing is their intense woodsy taste with a hint of apricots that makes the flavor of normal store-bought mushrooms fade to cardboard. Once you've tasted a chanterelle, you will always be on the lookout for them like my cousin Paul, who was enamored of these mushrooms and didn't realize he would encounter them when we went for a walk near our property. Unprepared to collect them, once he spotted these delectable chanterelles, he whipped off his baseball cap and filled it to overflowing.

It is the aromatic siren song of the chanterelle wafting into the lecture room that makes our upcoming dinner so appetizing. It reminds me of home-cooked meals that seduce with their aromas while simmering on the stove. Take-out food or dining in restaurants is like having sex without foreplay—there's no teasing, no anticipating the sensual delights to come that make you appreciate them all the more when they finally arrive. Margaret Mead once told her daughter, who was a busy college professor, that if she didn't have time to cook a full meal, at least make a pot of soup to fill the house up with its inviting cooking smells. But you don't have to be an anthropologist to figure out the important role of aromas in the home.

That's why I've never understood how people can be satisfied with gas fireplaces. Although they're convenient and imitate flames licking real logs, they lack an important element—the smell of burning wood. Once there is a chill in the air, I'm always eager to make wood fires because the charred incense they generate reminds me of so much: Girl Scout campfires in Maryland, replete with s'mores and ghost stories; wood fires in Maine used to boil lobsters at roadside stands or to keep us warm while we dressed in front of them on chilly mornings; campouts with college friends in Wisconsin gathered around the fire talking about past loves, future ambitions, and the meaning of it all while light flickered on our faces under a star-studded sky. All those layers of memory and meaning come back when sitting by a wood fire and taking in its smoky scent.

It was that special memory-inducing fragrance of Maine I was seeking while looking for a house there. After three days of searching on the Schoodic Peninsula, the real estate agent drives us down the gravel tree-lined driveway of one final property she had on her list. I am immediately entranced by an evocative scent that takes me back to a forested shore and a four-year-old version of myself skittering from boulder to cobble, plucking the whelks and periwinkles crowning them. Younger versions of my parents and brother also surface. My father's gray hair fades in my mind and turns back to black. His shirt pocket once more holds his ever-present slide rule and mechanical pencil. My mother's wrinkles smooth and the bitterness drains from her caramel-colored eyes. My bald and bearded brother is no longer withering in a wheelchair but has a Dennis-the-Menace haircut whose cowlick bounces along with each bounding step he takes. We are picnicking at Pretty Marsh while watching the rapidly ripening sun slide down between converging lines of conifers on the cliff above the water. I have to dodge the cones Joe keeps throwing at me until our parents banish both of us to the bay, where we skip rocks on the shore, competitively counting how many splashes our stones make.

After the real estate agent opens the carved mahogany door of the house and I smell the charred remains of logs in the large fireplace, there my family is again in front of a smoky fire warming us during a nor'easter storm whipping its way through the area. Afraid of the wind crying in the chimney, I cower in my mother's lap. Sheets of water pour out of overfilled gutters and rhythmically pound the ground while we work on a jigsaw puzzle, which, unlike those of latter years, has no pieces missing.

These memories come rushing back because the aroma of the property has just the right proportion of pine, cedar, and fir scents mixed in with that of mud, mussels, and woodsmoke. Like a bloodhound tracking a scent trail, I followed this distinctive heady bouquet until it led me to what would soon become our new Maine home. I am giddy about the possibilities it would offer for the past to become present, for my family to be together again, and for my child self, full of wonder, to step forward and reclaim her territory.

The nose knows.

CHAPTER FOUR

Naming Nature

Adam gave names to all cattle, and to the fowl of the air, and to
every beast of the field.

—Genesis 2:20

Every animal encountered when I was a child was befriended
and given a name. The occasional earthworm surfacing during
rainstorms was always named Wormy and provided delightful entertainment on dreary days. Crouching in rain boots, I watched
Wormy slither a slimy path across the sidewalk. After picking him up
and encasing him in my palm, Wormy travelled home to my yard where
he became a pet for the day. During the first hot and humid days of
summer, fireflies (also named) were flashy friends collected and put into
a glass jar so they could keep me company and pierce the scary darkness
with their luminescence before I fell asleep. Further up the vertebrate
scale, there were the guinea pig companions, Muffy and Scruffy, and the
beagle-dachshund mutt, Moxie, who understood everything confessed
to her and licked the tears off my face.

With a brother so much older that he frequently wasn't interested
in sharing my childish games, I was a somewhat solitary child. There
were children on the block with whom I could play, but I was unable
to ace the fine art of socializing. My paltry social finesse combined with
an inability to keep an eye on the ball made me the last kid picked for
softball teams at school. While I looked down at the ground, kicking
the dirt in the ball field, the captains of each team alternated picking
their players, choosing those most athletic first, the rest named in order
of their popularity. But the animals always accepted me, even if I still

wore saddle shoes when loafers were in, and even if I was oblivious to the social games you have to play to make friends.

Once entering adolescence, the folly of anthropomorphizing animals became apparent, and I spent more time with my human counterparts, swept up into dances, dates, and the drama of high school dynamics, in which friends could quickly become fiends if you do not follow numerous unstated rules inherent in claustrophobic teenaged tribes. But I never lost fascination for animals and the other worlds in which they dwelled—the twisted underground burrows of woodchucks, the papery hives of wasps, the underwater kelp forests of fish, and the overarching sky where hawks soar in wind currents and geese imprint their black chevrons each fall. I collected shed snakeskins, lost feathers, abandoned shells, and any other mementos of other beings, other worlds. These collections, which overflowed every window ledge, expanded my limited view and served as a reminder that there is more out there, *so much more*, hiding in plain sight.

Like the bird I have been playing hide-and-seek with for nearly fifteen minutes and which is currently lodged in the maple tree above the deck. Having just settled down to a steaming brew of espresso, originally intending to focus on the distant line of conifers that define the edge of the bay, something caught my eye much closer—the flitting of this small bird who first announced its presence by moving the tree leaves in front of me. As soon as I focus my binoculars on the feathered flurry, it disappears, only to resurface behind a new patch of shaking leaves, tantalizing me with a colorful bit of its anatomy—a yellow throat or an olive wing streaked with gray.

I frantically flip through the bird book to find it, but that proves futile. Although patting myself on the back for astutely noticing all that I could in a few fleeting glimpses, inevitably the one feature that distinguishes the bird from all its close cousins is the one feature I neglect to see or, more likely, neglect to notice—who would think its streaked breast mentioned in the bird book was key?

And so the hide-and-seek game starts all over again. *Come on, show me some breast*, I beseech the bird like a lecher at a peep show, and by now the coffee has turned as cold as the chill morning air in Maine that envelopes it.

What does it matter if it's a pine warbler or a Cape May warbler? Either way, it's just a bird. But I am determined to identify *this bird* because, being new to the neighborhood, I want to know my neighbors.

It is the first summer at our home in Maine, a glass-walled house lodged in a forest with a rocky beach for a backyard. Evergreen boughs stretch out over the quarter-mile-long gravel driveway. Cedars, firs, pines, and spruces also surround the house on three sides, providing plenty of perches for the many species of birds that fly by, including bald eagles, warblers, and thrushes. Further adding to the avian diversity is the seascape behind the house, which is ever-changing due to the extreme tides in Down East Maine. High tide brings floating lines of eider ducks, fishing cormorants, and seagulls that cling to the last remaining rocks above water. At low tide, herons, yellowlegs, and plovers stab fish in the tide pools or probe the seaweed and mud.

People are few and far between.

Our closest human neighbors are a ten-minute walk away, and it takes twenty minutes to drive to the few storefronts comprising the closest town. When Frank and I told our Philadelphia friends of our plan to spend the entire summer in Maine, where the only skyscrapers are giant spruces and the closest decent restaurant or movie theater is an hour's drive away, many looked aghast at our plan to "live in the middle of nowhere," as they put it. Although eager to experience a more natural environment, I shared some of their trepidation about being so far removed. Would we survive without plays and symphonies, museums and galleries, ethnic restaurants and library lectures? Would we miss that buzz and hum of the human hive? How could we live in one area for so long with "nothing to see or do"?

To many of us immersed in the city, nature is a monolithic backdrop with no distinguishing features, a solid-colored curtain that offers no way near the drama of the human play that unfolds before it. We don't see the twisted bark of the cedar or hear the haunting flute-like song of the thrush. We don't notice the ants carting away their dead under our feet or spot the nuthatch above crawling up a tree. In the city, the human is the only species in our world, except for maybe the dog or cat and occasional robin. We've lost the ability to experience the bustling biodiversity around us.

To some degree, I too had on city blinders, like the horses that pull the carriages for historic tours of Philadelphia. To avoid the stress of overstimulation, I had become accustomed to tuning out much of what I saw while visiting the city—the plethora of people passing by, the storefronts filled with merchandise, and the buildings that loom toward each other when you look up, blotting out the sky.

Such complexity of the city can be overwhelming unless we temper what we absorb. Nature too is complicated, but our eyes and brains are designed to process the type of branching complexity often seen in a natural environment. Such fractal patterns have large forms regularly echoed by smaller similar shapes within them—think of a tree and all its branches—and are prevalent in such artistic natural wonders as intricate crystalline snowflakes, the feathered frost that forms on a windowpane, blossoming flowers and clouds, and spiraling galaxies. Fractal patterns also can be found in artificial environments but usually at a level of complexity beyond what naturally resonates with our retinas, which process what we see. This helps explain why cities can be both stimulating and exhausting. We must exert more energy to visually process a cityscape compared to a natural landscape.

The loud noises the city belches continually are also taxing. Honking horns, clanging and jackhammering of construction workers, and blasts of passing buses all can induce a stress response that raises our blood pressure and makes us breathe faster. It's no wonder that many people try to replace these city sounds with music coming from their earbuds, a form of learned deafness, Florence Williams noted in her book *The Nature Fix*. "We are tuning out the real world in favor of our own personal soundscapes," she wrote, which is especially salient given more people live in urban than in rural environments worldwide.

Now in Maine, I'm starting to remove the city blinders and be more attentive to the natural sounds and sights around me, realizing there is much to see, hear, and even smell "in the middle of nowhere." There's no exhibit to see at a museum, but here I can spot a porcupine meandering onto the lawn or a field resplendent with the indigo stalks of wild lupines in bloom. There's no symphony performance to attend, but I can enjoy the staccato patter of rain on the roof or the operatic overtures of seals and seagulls in the bay. And the food aromas mixed with the odors of car exhaust that emanate from the city have been replaced by the scents of seaweed, mud, and forest all mixed together. I can smell my childhood.

Not that I fully experience what is around me at first.

I have to train my eye to distinguish the plump form of the plover from the more streamlined shape of the sandpiper, my ear to hear the eerie call of the loon versus the loud peeping of the osprey, and my nose to distinguish the spicy smells of pines from the more pungent scents of firs. A good way to overcome obliviousness to all the wildlife around us is to observe and to name it. When we fine-tune our naming—calling one bird a red-headed woodpecker and another a downy woodpecker— we actually see the red head versus the black-and-white head of the two species. We see twice as much by making these verbal distinctions. It is necessary to know if it's a Cape May warbler or a pine warbler, just like it is necessary to know whether it's Susan or Mary seen at a party in Philadelphia. By knowing such distinctions, our world is enriched with double the amount of perception, double the number of friends.

Sometimes language can spotlight fine distinctions in nature we wouldn't otherwise notice. In certain regions of Great Britain, there are words for nuances in the landscape most of us wouldn't notice. For example, the Scottish have a word—*caochan*—for a slender moor stream so obscured by vegetation that it's virtually hidden from sight. And in some English communities, *smeuse* is the word for the gap in the base of a hedge made by the regular passage of a small animal. Knowing that word now, I'm going to look for holes in hedges and the bitty beasts they might herald.

The Oxford University Press recently sparked a controversy when its 2008 edition of the *Oxford Junior Dictionary* removed many of its word entries dealing with natural elements in our world, such as *acorn*, *newt*, and *ivy*, to make room for what it deemed children were more likely to encounter—*chatroom*, *cut-and-paste*, and *voice-mail*. The nature writer Robert Macfarlane bemoaned these changes, noting "the outdoor and the natural being displaced by the indoor and virtual," he wrote in *The Guardian*. Emerson once called on writers to "pierce rotten diction and fasten words again to visible things," but Macfarlane noted, "The terrain beyond the city fringe is chiefly understood in terms of large generic units (*field, hill, valley, wood*)." It has become a "blandscape," making us indifferent to the distinction among the features found in the natural world. Such "a language deficit leads to attention deficit," Macfarlane cautioned.

A language deficit also can affect our understanding of the world around us. People who experience damage to the part of the brain devoted to noticing and naming distinctions in the world not only can't tell apart two different species of woodpeckers, they can't tell a kangaroo from an ostrich. As Carol Yoon noted in her book *Naming Nature*, "These are people completely at sea. Without the power to order and name life, a person simply does not know how to live in the world, how to understand it. How to tell the carrot from the cat—which to grate and which to pet? They are utterly lost, anchorless in a strange and confusing world."

I've seen the importance of naming with my almost two-year-old, towheaded great-nephew Ethan, whom the family calls "the Narrator." Though limited in vocabulary, he continually names what he sees and hears—Tami's car; plane flying; bells ringing; dog barking. It's a non-stop verbal panoply of the world around him, a perpetual blog that helps fine-tune his seeing and hearing and brings into focus what once was a confusing blur of sensations. Because to order and name life is to have a sense of the world around, and, as a result, what one's place is in it. Is it not telling that one of the first things biblical Adam does after entering the world's stage is to name all the animals around him?

Naming also can provide connection between us and those whose names we utter. We may say the names of those no longer with us so they linger before lumbering off into the oblivion of death. The names of the newly departed are spoken at every Jewish service, and those who died more than a year ago have their names spoken on each anniversary of their deaths. Once my friend Terry came to visit me in Maine a few years after her twenty-six-year-old son Jeremiah died from cancer. It was a warm day, so we walked to the nearby sandy beach and I waded into the frigid water, flinching at every icy wave that splashed me. Wiser than I, Terry chose instead to feel the cool breeze along the shore without delving into the shockingly cold temperatures of the water that created it. But unlike most people who comb the beach, dawdling to pick up glimmering sea glass or an abandoned whelk shell, she was striding with a steadfast gait. After coming out of the ocean and drying off, I caught up with Terry, who no longer had her usual smile but instead looked almost distraught, as if she were a fisherman's wife pacing the shoreline while waiting for her husband's boat to return after a storm.

"Are you okay?" I asked her.

"I'm fine," Terry said, rubbing one of her eyes.

She asked me how my swim was, our chatter superficial, the smile back on her face. It was only later as we were sitting by the bay drinking a glass of wine and talking about a friend of mine who had just lost his thirty-year-old daughter that Terry divulged she had spent the entire time I was swimming reciting Jeremiah's name over and over like a mantra. "You get to mention Jake's name all the time when you talk to your friends and family, but I rarely get to say Jeremiah's," she said. "So I make up for it by saying his name when I have my private moments."

It was then that I realized the necessity of naming not only what is around you, but those who can no longer be found despite persistent seeking. I too have felt this need when seeing my sister-in-law Elke, and despite the tears it may elicit, we reminisce about Joe and my parents and for a brief period of time, calling up their names and the memories attached to them brings them back into our present family fold, completes who is at our kitchen table. To name is to know, to know and not forget.

Rabbis at funerals often mention the gift of memory that enables a lost loved one to live on in the minds of others long after they are gone. I heard a rabbi say this at a funeral recently, along with something else that continued to resonate: the loss of a loved one is like a gaping hole in a web of supportive connections, so everyone who is in that web should come closer to patch the hole.

I want the animals to come closer.

Like that bird that is still hiding from me in the maple tree. *Come out from behind those leaves please—I just want to know your name!*

CHAPTER FIVE

More Than Meets the Eye

Attention is the beginning of devotion.

—Mary Oliver

It is a disembodied voice from the heavens. But unlike the imperial voice of God, this voice has a distinctive Maine accent. "I can see it *ov-ah they-ah*," it says. Then another disembodied voice answers, "I *gottit*."

Where are those voices coming from? It is high tide so they couldn't have come from clammers, who arrive only when the bay is a mudflat. Neighbors perhaps? But our neighbors live too far away to overhear their conversation so clearly. Scanning the bay with binoculars, I see them—far across the water, in a skiff, are two small figures. Dressed in green rubber boots and yellow mackintoshes, these gentlemen are busy pulling up lobster traps. They have no idea that I—a mere pinprick on their horizon—can hear every word they say.

Sounds travel far on the bay.

The sea spoke to me once when I was a small child scampering along the water's edge and a large intact whelk shell tumbled out of the ocean and landed next to my bare feet. Picking up this labyrinthine treasure, I ran back to show my mother. *If you put the seashell to your ear, you can hear the sea*, she told me. Doing so, I was startled by the whooshing roar of the vast ocean somehow captured inside a small shell. How could that be? What was the sea's message?

Later I learned that when you hear that rushing sound inside a seashell, you are probably not hearing the ocean, but rather sounds in the environment bouncing around inside the shell's spiraled structure.

The seashell is merely a resonance chamber that makes you more aware of sounds around you. So perhaps this is the message the sea was sending: *Listen.*

It's easy to heed that message while in Maine because, akin to the whelk shell, the bay also amplifies ambient sounds and makes you more cognizant of them. Normally sound does not travel loudly very far because it is dispersed in so many different directions, radiating out like a cone from its point of origin. But due to a trick of physics, the bay's cooler surface air, compared to the air above it, acts as a channel for sound that prevents it from dispersing, sending it like a laser beam across the water. Such concentrated sound enables me to eavesdrop on the conversations of fishermen and seals miles away, as well as to notice other sounds not ordinarily heard. Especially intrigued by the unfamiliar sounds encountered at my Maine abode, I want to uncover what makes them, recognizing that one way to make the acquaintance of new neighbors—both the wild animals and the tamed humans—is to listen to what they have to say.

Sounds don't have to travel far to reach me in Philadelphia's suburbs because they are omnipresent. I enjoy spending time outdoors, so on our Philly suburban house we built a deck that could serve as an outdoor office when the weather was nice. I hoped to read there while being serenaded by birds. But every time I plopped down into the Adirondack chair on the deck, leaf blowers blared, chain saws buzzed, lawn mowers droned, or Led Zeppelin shouted from the radios of roofers or other outdoor workmen. After being so aurally assaulted, I slunk back indoors, once more frustrated by attempts to immerse myself in the kind of nature the suburbs had to offer.

The need for quiet, or at least for more natural sounds, made the prospect of summers in Maine especially appealing. Finally I would hear myself think again without any jarring auditory intrusions. I could dwell on the meaning behind the matter, the new narrative I needed to write about myself and my family now that most of its members were gone. When you undergo a major life change, the garment you have knitted together from important strands of your life—the story you told yourself—no longer fits and you have to knit a new one. But weaving this novel narrative requires blending your recent experiences with those from the past—a parent's last breath melds into the first cry of a son or daughter; a herd of butterflies or a harrowing kayak ride twines with a memory of a grandmother or an end-of-life discussion with a brother. All of these strands can spool from a profound place in the mind when there are no noisy distractions that inadvertently cause you to drop a stitch or forget the overall pattern. I looked forward to entering this more meditative and tranquil realm, reveling in the sounds of nature.

Fat chance.

The first summer in Maine we are awakened every morning at around 5:00 a.m. by the low-pitched but loud puttering of lobster boats. Many of these small, motorized crafts weave about our bay, checking their traps in summer. Because of the way the bay channels the noise they make, these boats sound like they are right underneath our bedroom windows.

Another woman "from away" subjected to the same early-morning alarm clock on the bay was the talk of the town one year. She bought a summer home in nearby Winter Harbor because of its picturesque view of the boats in the water with the pink granite mountains of Acadia a backdrop. But she didn't realize that Winter Harbor is a working harbor, not just a place for pleasure boats and photographers.

In our part of Maine, it starts getting light out around 4:00 a.m. in summer. Even before those first rays of sun sparkle the water, boats leave the harbor so lobstermen can fish in the early morning hours when waters are calmer. Consequently, this woman in Winter Harbor was disturbed early every morning by loud thrumming. She complained to the town office, requesting that lobster boats not be permitted to leave the harbor until a much later hour in the morning so that she could sleep in.

Keep in mind that lobster fishing is the primary industry in Maine. So asking lobstermen to alter their work hours here is like asking Wall Street brokers in New York City to do the same—it ain't gonna happen. The town office ignored the woman's request, of course, but word about it traveled far and wide. For the next few weeks in the wee hours of the morning, every local lobsterman made a point of tooting his boat's horn—a note of welcome, so to speak—as he puttered past this woman's home.

From the puttering of lobster boats to the cries of the seagulls that follow them, the sounds of a place paint a picture of the landscape as vivid as the colors, shapes, and textures that reach our eyes and in some cases reveal more. Bioacoustician Bernie Krause has been recording soundscapes from the natural world since 1968, from coral reefs to the Amazon rainforest. Sadly, half of the more than two thousand habitats he has recorded no longer exist, their recorded soundscapes all that remain.

In an era before tape recorders, Aldo Leopold, the father of wildlife conservation, took such detailed notes about when and where on his property each bird species began to sing that decades later my University of Wisconsin avian ecology professor used those notes like a musical score. In 2010, working with digital recordings of birdsong from Cornell University's Lab of Ornithology, Stan Temple re-created the soundscape at Leopold's shack on the morning of June 1, 1940.

Since that time, an interstate was put in near Leopold's property and farms were turned into housing developments, causing many original birds to vanish, their songs replaced by man-made noise. "I think people are increasingly aware of how pervasive human-generated sound has become," Temple said in an article from the University of Wisconsin Alumni Association magazine, "so it's refreshing to be able to hear a more natural soundscape from the past."

Refreshing, perhaps, but it's also a little uncanny to take a plunge back in aural time. Kind of like visiting Williamsburg and seeing streets filled with women wearing hoop skirts and shawls and men walking around in droll knickers and stockings. There's a disturbing sense of unreality to it all. At the same time, it was also unsettling for me to hear the more contemporary recordings of the male lyrebird of the Australian rainforests. The lyrebird is known for its incredible ability to imitate within its own song as many as twenty different melodies from other bird species. But sadly, as development has impinged on their habitat, some lyrebirds have taken to imitating man-made sounds, including camera shutter clicks, blaring car alarms, and the buzzing of chain saws felling trees. There is a tragic irony in a bird that can sing the song of the chain saw that is destroying its world.

After those first encounters with the lobster boats, I realize, like a child forced to give up her make-believe play, that I'd never be Eve back in Eden—it's not possible to go back to a time before the hum of motors or the clanging or buzzing of machinery. Instead, with the heightened awareness of a newcomer, I devote myself to exploring the Maine soundscape, which is so vastly different than the one left behind in Philadelphia, revealing critters you can't see because they are hidden by foliage or only come out under the cloak of darkness.

This shoreline symphony, while not idyllic, still provides its own pleasures and unique players you can come to know by sound. At first, the score in summer is a babel of multiple animal dispatches overwhelming in complexity and foreignness. But I learn to dissect the cacophony with the help of field guidebooks and websites. The loud and repetitive "pick me, pick me, pick me" trills come from tiny courting warblers hidden in trees, I discover, while the buzzing, old-fashioned, alarm-clock calls are the sound trademarks of red squirrels. Every morning a flock of nuthatches nasally honk their ritual daybreak chants like monks with bad colds. I heard them weeks before seeing these small slate-and-rust-colored birds climbing up tree trunks and branches, defying gravity. Occasionally you can hear the loud knocking of a pileated woodpecker that compels you to look up and wonder, *Who's there?*

And of course there are the indignant noises of seagulls. These birds perch on evenly spaced boulders that zigzag along the shore. When a newcomer flies into the bay looking for a dry place to land, each seagull raucously defends its rocky promontory as the new bird approaches. This triggers a screeching symphonic echo that gets fainter as the intruding bird flies further down the bay. There's nothing melodic about the sounds seagulls make, but I've come to appreciate the sea vistas those screeches evoke—the gulls' vocalizations are intricately tied to scenes from the bay.

The loons are another story.

Their sonorous lamentations remind me of my own mortality, as if they were John Donne's bells tolling. But the loon has a different auditory side that is less haunting. Its tremolo chortle, which it uses as a warning cry, sounds like the nervous giggle of a teenage girl. One day, while listening to Vivaldi's *Four Seasons* on the radio, these throaty calls made by several loons on the bay seep through our window screens. Wanting to hear them better, I turn the radio off, but then their chortling stops. Perhaps the loons are responding to the calls of Vivaldi's violins? Birds react to birdsongs in the same way that people react to music—it activates the portion of their brains responsible for triggering emotional reactions, brain scans reveal. And perhaps because of strong connections between the sound and motor processing regions in their brains, akin to what is seen in humans, some pet birds, like the internet sensation Snowball the cockatoo, bob to the beat of popular music heard on the radio. Can soundtracks be a universal language that transcends the borders of some species? I do not respond amorously to the desperate trills of a courting warbler, but I do appreciate his melodic missive, so maybe in some similar way Vivaldi is able to speak to loons?

The loons certainly speak to me, along with many of the other animals on our coast. Even the marine mud has something to say. After years of pairing sounds to sights, I've learned the soundscape of this rocky shore and can translate the messages it sends: The loud swishing in the air overhead means a bald eagle is flapping its wings on its way to its eyrie; a raspy cry signals a heron flying by. The combination of splashing and wing flapping nearby denotes the emergence of high tide and eider ducks preening themselves in water close to shore. Low tide offers a different concert. If you crouch down close to the seabed, you actually can hear the tinkling-popping sounds of water being sucked from the mudflat. Those are the sounds of the moon in action.

At low tide you also can hear the far-off, low-pitched growls of seals lounging on the rocks, which sound like a cross between pirates' *aarrghs* and empty stomach rumblings. These growls crescendo when the tide comes in. Then a small boulder in the bay that is a favorite way station for seals gradually disappears into the water, creating a survival-of-the-fittest battle. That battle is really the survival of the loudest, because each seal defends its perch by growling louder than the others and by using its flippers to slap any seals that try to flop out of the water onto the rock.

More melodic are the haunting flute-like serenades of the wood thrushes at sunset. Often a few at different locations will take turns singing their series of loud, lilting notes, which seem to come from everywhere at once. These stirring arias, combined with the ethereal shafts of late-day light penetrating the forest, are akin to hearing a choir singing in a place of worship as sunbeams enter high windows, spotlighting the faithful.

Night blindness, and perhaps some innate fears and ancient superstitions, makes you more acutely aware of sounds at night. When our two children were small, we rented a small cabin by the bay in Maine enclosed on three sides by the forest. We relished our privacy and solitude—*Yeah to no neighbors! Yeah to no clothes!*—until one night when we were awakened by the sounds of two men talking. Being from the big city, we envisioned the worst—robbers, murderers, or rapists. Irrational fears flourished in the dark, multiplying like a choking invasive weed. Every horror movie ever watched rushed to the foreground of our minds. We started looking around the cabin for something to offer us protection—a broom, a hammer, a dull kitchen knife? The choices were meager.

But then we followed the pattern of flashlights on the shore and realized the men we heard were walking far out on the mudflat in front of our cabin. And we remembered that some men had come two days earlier and asked if they could access our bay to gather some clams. We didn't realize they would show up at three o'clock in the morning when it was pitch dark, but apparently it was low tide then and these clammers were just doing their job. We heaved a huge sigh of relief and went back to sleep, thankful for futures that had been blissfully restored.

There are still moments when I fear the strange sounds heard outdoors in the dark. The first summer at our Maine house, soon after the light dimmed, I heard rough scratching sounds, followed by a rustling of leaves and plopping sounds. With no idea what could be making these noises, I imagined everything from moose to murderers.

Then one day around sunset, I saw a porcupine shinnying the maple tree outside our deck, its claws scraping the bark loudly (*scratch*). Once it got to a comfortable perch in the crook of some limbs, the porcupine drew a nearby branch and its bunch of leaves into its mouth (*rustle*). This tree-side dining scattered a few small branches and leaves, which fell to the ground (*plop*). Sound mystery solved—I can see in my mind's eye what is making those sounds when hearing them at night.

Having learned to listen to and recognize what's around me, my world has expanded with animals and auditory rhythms in the bay that previously went undetected. The birdsongs, growling seals, water splashing, and other natural sounds sailing the airwaves are not jarring like many man-made sounds and instead seep into my inner thoughts in a much more subtle and soothing way. The wild soundscape provides a sound sanctuary, enabling the narrative within to resonate outward.

I desperately needed that sound sanctuary our fifth summer in Maine. That was the summer I drove up by myself, eager to be back after a difficult winter during which my father had died and we moved from the suburbs to a smaller place in the heart of Philadelphia so we could more easily attend the theater, dance, music, and other stimulating offerings there. That move required sifting the wheat from the chaff of possessions accumulated over twenty-five years lived in the same house and doing the same for what remained in my father's apartment. The decision making was nerve wracking. Do I throw out the boxes of scientific journal articles that were all that remained of my father's professional life? Do I keep my mother's recipe book, her distinctive slanted writing on every page? Do I read through their love letters and risk crumbling them in their unfolding? And what remnants do I keep of my children when they were small—Jake's Batman shirt that he wore nonstop when he was three, the curly blond lock of hair from Eva's first haircut, letters from camp?

Having completed this onerous task of deciding what should remain, as well as packing and emptying out both our house and my father's apartment, I yearned for a quiet space to mentally unpack. What does it mean to get rid of most of what reminds you of your parents, your children, or yourself as a parent or as a child? What are you left with? These were questions I needed to answer while gazing out at the bay.

Not willing to wait another week in Philadelphia while Frank finished up some projects there, I headed to Maine without him and arrived just before sunset, exhausted after a twelve-hour drive and ready to relax with a beer before unloading a car filled to the brim with clothes, books, and groceries. While wood thrushes sang their lovely melodies, I dug out the key to the house from my luggage, shook out the kinks in my limbs, and opened the door that was last closed eight months previously.

It was a door to disaster.

Something was wrong, I realized after first entering the house and not being greeted by the usual pleasant smell of the last wood fire we made combined with the earthy smells of cedar ceilings and leather furniture. Instead there is a foul, musty odor. Then I see an impressive slimy border of something seaweed-like on the baseboards leading out of the bathroom and down the hall. *How did kelp get inside the house?* There is also a furry lining of mold on the walls and a layer of black sludge on the bathroom floor that had oozed into the laundry room. There a dead red squirrel lies, its nest of leaves above a cabinet, as well as a few desiccated mice. With trepidation, I walk upstairs and find the floor carpeted with animal droppings along with broken seashells, sea glass, and stones. These sea treasures had previously adorned the windowsills and presumably were knocked down by another red squirrel whose dead body is now splayed on the office floor.

It is horrifying.

I like going back to nature every summer when we return to the Schoodic Peninsula but am shocked to discover that the house has done so in our absence. I feel violated by these unwanted and unexpected invasions into my Maine sanctuary. Once over the initial dismay, it becomes apparent to me that sometime in the spring while we were in Philadelphia, a malfunctioning septic system combined with heavy snowmelt must have caused sewage to seep into our house. This spurred the extensive growth of mold and kelp-like fungi I observed on the first floor. Coincidentally, squirrels and mice had broken in, probably through the laundry vent, and had scattered their droppings throughout the house before eating the animal poison we'd left that ultimately killed them.

Fortunately, my neighbors Larry and Mary are kind enough to give me a place to stay that first night, so I won't have to endure the awful smells and unhealthy spores. Even though tired from the long drive, I sleep fretfully, worrying how my home will ever be restored to normalcy. In this anxious state, I easily am awakened at 5:00 a.m. by the loud chugging of a lobster boat. It keeps rising in noise level and pitch as it travels toward another trap, then returns to a steadfast putter while the men aboard the boat pull up and unload the metal cages.

The sound soothes me.

It is as pleasing to the ears as the singsong voice of a warbler or the lullaby of a thrush. That's when I realize I have made the transition and become a true Mainer—I am no longer annoyed by the sound of the lobster boat. Instead its thrumming is comforting and tied to memories of sitting by the bay with morning coffee steaming, relaxed and inspired by that wide expanse of blue that dwarfs all problems, from mold overtaking the house to death overtaking my family. Like Pavlov's dogs, which were conditioned to drool at the sound of a bell that previously rang whenever they were fed, I, too, have linked the sound of the lobster boat to the expectation of receiving sustenance, although of a more spiritual nature.

I also have learned to hear the chugging of the lobster boat and the chatter of clammers as recurring refrains emblematic of the independent industriousness of people trying to live off the land (or should I say water?). Are the ambitious, albeit louder, efforts of these people any less a part of nature than those of terns dive-bombing for fish or seagulls dropping mussels from midair perches to break their shells on the rocks below? At the end of the day, we all have to eat, gathering food can sometimes be a noisy enterprise, and sounds travel far on the bay.

CHAPTER SIX

Unseen Worlds

For me, the microscope was like a pair of magic glasses that revealed the underlying nature of reality.

—Gary Greenberg, *A Grain of Sand: Nature's Secret Wonder*

It is dawn and steam from my mug of coffee twirls up into the heavens like a smoke signal to God that another soul has awoken grateful for a new day, a new vista—and for caffeine. After settling into the Adirondack chair by the bay, I pick up the binoculars dangling around my neck and take inventory of what is there. Seals balancing their bellies on rocks, tails and heads lifted so they look like smiles. Preening eiders that the natives call "skunk ducks" because of their black-and-white attire. Loons diving into water sparkled by the sun. Without binoculars, all these animals would have blurred into the blue sea, indistinguishable as the creatures that lie within it. Once, after peering into the high-powered scope a park ranger provided on a shorebird walk, dots across the water magically turned into hundreds of sandpipers, yellowlegs, and plovers poking their beaks in the low-tide mud.

What else am I missing?

My twenty-six-year-old son knows the value of lenses that open up new worlds. When he and the rest of the family converged on my sister-in-law's country home in Vermont last Thanksgiving, Jake brought his telescope so he could take advantage of being far from blinding city lights and air pollution. After our Thanksgiving feast, when we had somnolently sunk into the couch in front of the wood-burning stove, we heard Jake say, "Guys, you've got to come out and see this! It's awesome!" Despite our postprandial ennui and an accumulation of years that fostered the biblical notion "there's nothing new under the sun," we trudged outside, and with our breath smoking in the frigid air, took turns looking through the telescope.

The sky was full of surprises.

What seemed to be a large star turned out to be Saturn and its planar rings. Craters surfaced on the moon under the magnification of the lenses, and even the familiar North Star, Polaris, which I had known as a solitary entity since childhood multiplied into three stars. The more we looked through the lenses of the telescope, the more that was there.

Similarly, a stargazing party at an open field in the Schoodic part of Acadia National Park in Maine one clear night in September was an eye-opener. The park is one of the top ten places in the country to view the night sky because of its lack of light pollution. With no flamboyant moon to outshine shyer stars and no artificial lights in sight, about two dozen of us walked from the park building to a big open field edged with the dark silhouettes of coniferous trees. "Turn off your flashlights," the balding park ranger with a ponytail told us once we arrived. After the last light died, we were smothered in blackness so profound that the features of everything around us instantly vanished, those beside us defaced to forms, detail eroded from the landscape, only voices remained. How disturbing to have everything wiped off the blackboard, with nothing familiar to guide us. There was that primordial aloneness and fear one often feels when waking in the middle of the night surrounded by complete darkness with only one's thoughts echoing. But shortly, glowing stars started chalking their presence; the brightest first, until soon the sky was filled with starlight and the claustrophobia of the engulfing emptiness subsided.

It took a while for my eyes to adjust and make out the telescopes that several amateur astronomers had set up in the field. We took turns seeing what they could reveal. "That's Andromeda," an age-ripened voice said while I peered into his telescope and saw a glowing oval of light surrounded by a swirling halo of fainter speckles. "It's a galaxy 2.5 million light years away and has about a trillion stars in it," the voice added. *What did this amateur astronomer look like?* Imagination running wild with night blindness, I pictured him as a cross between Dumbledore and Merlin. Someone old, wise, and wizardly, with a magic telescope instead of a wand.

"A trillion?" I responded, not sure I heard him right. I thought there were only "billions and billions" of stars in the entire universe, as the astronomer Carl Sagan used to say on the television show I watched as a child. But in a neighboring galaxy there's a *trillion* stars? *How could I not have known this?!* I felt like I was three years old again and, having climbed the hill that filled our backyard and obstructed my view, discovered at its peak that I was surrounded by dozens of split-level houses just like mine.

When expressing my astonishment that Andromeda could contain so many stars, the voice replied, "Oh, that's nothing. There's lots more stars than that out there—if every grain of sand was a star and you took all the sand from all the beaches and deserts on the planet, they still wouldn't equal how many stars are out there in the universe." The voice also told me that Andromeda is one of our closest neighboring galaxies and, before its discovery, people assumed all the stars in the universe were bottled up in our own Milky Way galaxy. Now we know better. Experts estimate there are more than one hundred *billion* observable galaxies in the universe. Plus, there may be multiple universes we can't see, with yet even *more* galaxies and stars, each star likely to be circled by several planets, which can each have numerous moons. An endless unrolling carpet of worlds appeared before me and all I could think of was those lines from the hymn "Amazing Grace": *I once was lost but now I'm found, was blind but now I see.*

Even without a telescope, expert stargazers can see so much to which many of us are blind. After looking through the telescopes at Acadia, we bunched up around the park ranger, who told us what *he* saw up in the sky. While our breath frosted in the air, he used his laser beam to point out the Big Dipper—the star grouping in the midnight sky that most people can detect easily. But then he showed how the three stars comprising the Big Dipper's handle can be expanded to a star-studded outline of a bear. And there aren't just bears up there, but a whole menagerie—a swan, a bull, a crab, and a fish.

All sorts of drama are unfolding in the sky, which is chock-full of characters from Greek myths, though all I saw was white glitter against an inky backdrop. Apparently, I lack the imagination of those ancient

Greeks, not spending as many nights as these seafaring folks did looking up at stars and counting on them for navigation.

The sky the ancient Greeks saw is not actually the same sky we see, although most of its guidepost stars have not varied. Despite the dependable Big Dipper, the heavens are not static—new stars are continually born as old stars explode. Even our own sun will someday grow old and die, and many of the exploded stars we see today actually died thousands of years ago—it just took that long for their last messages of light to reach us.

One famous star explosion happened around 1000 AD. Eyeing the sky without the aid of any lenses, Chinese astronomers noticed a "guest star" suddenly appeared one night in the Taurus constellation and for two days was bright enough to read by it at night and even see it when the sun was out. That guest was the explosive dying gasp of a star that eventually left behind a stardust smudge in the sky known as the Crab Nebula.

One of the amateur astronomers at Acadia showed us this nebula, now a nursery for new stars. The smear of white speckles in the telescope wasn't that impressive until later, when cruising the internet, I found pictures of the same nebula taken by a much more powerful telescope. These pictures revealed an intricate tatting of stardust over a brilliant aqua blue background edged with orange. You think it is a black-and-white world up there, but with the right telescope and filters, you can see brilliantly colored displays in the nighttime sky. I felt like Dorothy entering the colorful land of Oz after leaving behind the black-and-white landscape of Kansas.

What else am I missing?

The infinity of the stars was almost too overwhelming to contemplate, let alone view, so I set my sights closer to the ground. Telescopes take you outward, but I wanted to journey inward. After Jake perused websites for just the right model, he sent me for Mother's Day something I had wanted for a long time—a microscope, my ticket to another world.

Dozens of ovoid creatures zip in and out of my magnified viewing circle. They tumble and spin in an amusing way like circus clowns on unicycles travelling in different directions. They are filled with sacks of green pigment—solar energy–tapping chlorophyll. I spend several minutes watching their comings and goings, entertained by their scattershot trajectories. Who would have known a single clear drop of water from a tidal pool in the bay could harbor so much commotion?

But these miniature bundles of energy aren't all. After moving the slide under the microscope, more beings come into view, including what looks like a mini spaceship because of its shape and the way it floats across the viewing screen. Its middle disk section is filled with two neighboring sacks of chartreuse and it is stretched out on both ends into long see-through spines. While admiring this spaceship slowly flying through microscopic space, a bright green, segmented worm-like critter undulates in and out of focus. More miniature spaceships appear. These too are transparent but don't have spines, although they have other remarkable features. One is outlined in yellow by a narrow tube filled with pigment and has regular lines gridding its otherwise clear body. Another is similarly rimmed with yellow, but more stretched out in shape, like a rubber band. Then an amber canoe-shaped critter glides its way across the viewing screen, followed by a particularly bizarre creature comprised of two perfectly shaped spheres, one honey-colored and the other completely clear. Both are encased in the same transparent capsule that has two parallel lines girding the middle.

Field guides confirm what I suspect—all these symmetrical forms are diatoms. They have elaborate spines and other ornamentation to enable them to stay afloat so they can absorb the sun's rays. I am intrigued by these newly discovered neighbors I didn't even realize I had. *Were they helpful or harmful? What kind of lives do they lead?*

Cruising the internet, I discover that diatoms are experts at creating something from nothing. Chemical magicians, they take silica dissolved in the surface of ocean water and concoct it into their crystalline cell walls, which are often etched with stunning intricate patterns due to the symmetrical way the crystals form. This dazzling silica shell better enables the diatom to perform its next act—to grab carbon dioxide in the air or water and turn it into a carbohydrate that fuels the microbe's existence. It does this amazing feat by using solar power it absorbs with its yellow, amber, or chartreuse pigments. The end result of all this chemical wizardry? The life-sustaining byproduct oxygen, on which many other creatures, including ourselves, rely. About half of our atmospheric oxygen comes from these photosynthesizing microbes hidden in the sea. Many sea animals, including mussels, lobster larvae, and the krill that feeds whales, also dine on these single-celled creatures.

Good neighbors, indeed.

(And from where does all that silica, which not only forms diatom shells, but sand grains and computer chips, come? Stardust. The high temperatures present when our solar system formed propelled elements of silicon—remnants of exploding stars—to bump into and then bind to those of oxygen. The resulting long-lasting unions, called silicates, comprise most of the earth's crust.)

Most diatoms just go with the flow, with no way of propelling themselves.

But dinoflagellates—the other creatures seen zipping around on the slide—can actively move thanks to their tails whirling them about. A dinoflagellate has two tails—one that trails it and propels it forward and another that encircles it and acts more like a rudder, enabling it to turn. The combined action of both tails comically whips the microbe forward like a slowly spinning top.

Dinoflagellates can be helpful or harmful neighbors. Some produce a paralyzing nerve toxin that can sicken or kill fish and shellfish and make the humans who dine on them quite ill. Large blooms of dinoflagellates form when warm weather combines with an influx of nutrients, often from pollutants. This causes the red tides that make ocean foods toxic. But the kinder face of the dinoflagellate comes from its more common ability to play well with others. Jellyfish, sponges, coral, and many other marine organisms swallow but don't digest dinoflagellates, which generously provide sun-derived food for these creatures in exchange for a safe harbor. This symbiotic exchange echoes the organism's evolutionary past, as the sacks of chlorophyll inside dinoflagellates probably were derived from diatoms once ingested by these tailed microbes.

Similarly, each of our cells has the remnants of ancient sea bacteria that still carry out vital roles. When life was new on Earth and found only in oceans, these bacteria entered the cells of larger single-celled microbes in search of food, like hungry feral cats entering a home to lap up milk in a bowl. Once inside, the bacteria became accustomed to their new cellular abodes and took up permanent residence in their hosts, who provided them with sustenance and kept them safe from predators. Eventually, these bacterial invaders rewarded their hosts by evolving into the mitochondria organelles that generate the energy cells need to function.

The sea has seeped into our bodies. Not only do its saline streams run in our coursing network of veins and arteries, but each of our cells harbors the relatives of ancient saltwater denizens that sustain us with their molecular manna.

One of the oldest still-living sea creatures I see under the microscope is a microbe so primitive that it has features of both plants and animals. I admire the immobile emerald necklaces made from these circular blue-green algae cells strung together. Other tubular strands of algae have green circles stuck like stickers on the outer margins of their clear cylindrical cells.

So this is what the clams and mussels in my bay eat—a beautiful buffet of algae, diatoms, and dinoflagellates. Who would have thought they had such spectacular fodder? Foodstuff that appears like aliens from another planet—or at least from another world. My plate of greens, potatoes, and chicken looks drab by comparison. But then again, maybe it wouldn't look so quotidian if I viewed these food offerings with magnification. I certainly never expected to find such magnificent jewels and spinning tops within a clear drop of water.

How much of the world we miss by not observing what is right in front of us, and how much more expansive our lives can be if we tune in to everything out there. I have lost a mother and brother, much of that first small familial sphere in which I was encased as a child, but that first day with the microscope, I dive into a single drop of water from the bay and break through to an entire new world I have never seen before, and it is like finally taking a deep breath after inhaling shallow sips for years. I find it hard to tear myself away and reenter the macroscopic realm. I yearn to keep spying on the miniature denizens. As Annie Dillard described her encounters with the microscopic world in *Pilgrim at Tinker Creek*, "These are real creatures . . . leading real lives, one by one. I can't pretend they're not there." I am like Dr. Seuss's Horton who hears a Who, and I no longer feel alone with so many zillions of creatures beside me. Instead I feel the need to champion their existence—to shout out their presence to others.

I e-mail Jake pictures of what I see under the microscope, but I get a rather lukewarm response.

"It's really cool, Mom, but how do you feel about swimming with all those microbes?" he g-chats to me.

"Fine," I type back. "It's not like they're all bad for you—we depend on many to digest our food and there are plenty of bacteria in our gut or on our skin all the time—we just can't see them."

A minute later the words "No, that's not true!" appear on my laptop screen, followed by, "*You* can see them!"

There is a way to see beneath the sea and glimpse the infinity of the miniature creatures within it without the aid of special lenses. But you have to do it on a dark night unperturbed by moonlight. If you're lucky, your naked eye can spot microbes akin to those I saw in the bay water under the microscope because these organisms emit light when jostled.

Karen, our tour guide for our night kayak ride in Castine, Maine, is a fit woman with a long black French braid just starting to go gray. While we sign release forms in her cedar shack office, she enchants us with luminous tales. "One time I went swimming at night and each step into the water created saucers of light around my feet," she tells Frank and me, another couple, and two young women. "Just the movement of your paddle in the water will create sparks."

Sparks in water? Surely fire cannot exist within water?

She explains that many dinoflagellates—those ovoid creatures with tails zipping around under my microscope like circus clowns—have an enzyme that makes a phosphorescent glow. It is the same enzyme that makes fireflies light up. Karen tells us you can see a lot of bioluminescence in the nutrient-rich portions of the bay in Castine we'll be exploring, but it's also common in most oceans and bays.

"Of course, it changes day to day—sometimes we see lots of bioluminescence and some nights we don't see much of anything," Karen says. We walk over to the dock, where she outfits each double and single kayak we're about to use with a tiny red light, equips us with life jackets, a whistle, and paddle, and explains how to maneuver the kayak and what to do if it capsizes.

By the time Frank and I enter our double kayak, the sun has set and a few stars and the planet Venus start to surface in the sky. We set out of the harbor, dodging pleasure boats anchored in the water. The bay is so calm it mirrors the stars emerging in the sky above, enveloping us in a sparkling vastness.

Once away from the lights on the dock, it becomes so dark that only the rough outlines of the other double kayaks and the red lights that dot their helms can be seen. But we can hear Karen, who maintains a banter to reassure us. "I've had lots of scientists go on this kayak tour, including a marine biologist who told me nobody really knows why there's bioluminescence in the ocean. They all have their theories—some say the plankton do it to startle their predators or to make visible the bigger critters trying to eat them, who will then be seen and eaten by even bigger fish. But no one really knows."

The water is calm and there is a still coolness in the air that makes me thankful I wore my sweatshirt. Frank and I continue to paddle, but no sparks emerge. Could we be kayaking on one of those nights when the bioluminescence is bland?

"One time I had a Mars geologist," Karen continues. "He's one of those guys who controls the exploring robot on Mars."

This reminds me of the oceanographer Robert Ballard, who discovered the sunken *Titanic*, and once commented that half of the United States lies under water, but we have better maps of Mars than we do of the underwater real estate in our own country. Another oceanographer, Sylvia Earle, pleads that we do more exploring of the ocean, 95 percent of which we have yet to see. Which is surprising given that nearly all of the living space in our planet is *in* the ocean, according to marine biologist Edith Widder. She also pointed out that it's not just microscopic plankton, but most animals in the sea that emit light. Consequently, the ocean "is a magical place filled with breathtaking light shows and bizarre and wondrous creatures, alien life forms that you don't have to travel to another planet to see," she said in a TED talk.

There is no moon and we're traveling at a steady clip, despite the fact that it is pitch black. I can't see the other kayakers, just their tiny red boat lights. These lights on Karen's kayak keep us on course, as well as her instructions. She guides us to a narrow shallow stretch of the bay where the phosphorescent plankton is supposed to be especially prevalent. But her general directions do little to calm my nervousness due to night blindness. "Keep to the left here or you might hit a rock," she calls out, and Frank adjusts his steering, narrowly missing a boulder, making me shudder. "Be careful—the bay is shallow here because of a sandbar," she says a little later, and I imagine us getting stuck. *How can you be careful when you can't see anything?*

But then I see them.

Lighting the commotion of our motion, sparks swirl off our paddles like dozens of shooting stars. I put my hand into the water and catch a few of the dancing lights. "Oh, wow!" I say. "I didn't expect them to be so big!"

"Yeah, they clump together," Karen says, "Maybe because of the silt in the water. And if you see larger circles of light, they're probably copepods—tiny bioluminescent crustaceans. The fish that eat them collect their light in their gills and then *they* start to glow."

I stop paddling and put my hand in the water as Frank continues to propel us forward. Each finger sends off a stream of sparkles akin to the glitter given off by Tinkerbell flying or the Good Witch of the North's magic wand.

We have been transported to another world.

"It is as if they wanted to lure the enchanted observer into a realm of fairies," one person wrote about his encounter with phosphorescent creatures in the sea in a letter from 1853.

I certainly am enchanted and back-paddle to splash harder and spark more of these fireflies of the sea, but Frank starts to complain that I'm slowing us down and we're too far behind the group. So I compromise, submerging a few fingers, mesmerized by the trail of light that follows them. We catch up with Karen, who guides us back to the pier. It's quiet and dark except for a bar called Dennett's. After we pull the kayaks up onto the dock and before returning our equipment, Karen asks us for feedback.

"So whad'ya think, guys? Was it what you expected?"

"It was *more* than I expected!" I say, and one of the young women adds, "We saw things out there most people will never see."

"I know what you mean," Karen responded. "One night I was the only one out kayaking the bay. Not only were there lots of stars and bio-luminescence, but the northern lights were dancing across the sky. But everyone was drinking inside Dennett's bar and missed it all! I wanted to shout to them 'Come out and see this, guys! You're missing the great-est show on Earth!'"

A few days after the kayak tour, I tell my friend Art about our aston-ishing encounter with bioluminescent plankton. Art is a lobster-man who fishes in our bay much of the year. "Oh yeah, I see those sparks in the water every time I oar back from my boat if it's late and already dark. I see it all the time."

He sees it all the time. In *our* bay. What else am I missing?

CHAPTER SEVEN

Fog

Nature reserves some of her choice rewards for days when her mood may appear to be somber.

—Rachel Carson, *The Sense of Wonder*

We bought our place in Maine because we were captivated by its view of three bays converging into an expansive stretch of water. It is the opposite of the Philadelphia suburb I had lived in for twenty years, where neocolonial homes spaced a few yards apart block both horizon and sky, usurping any sense of open space. Finally there would be a big vista accompanied by the exhilarating sense that anything is possible, including creative mental journeys unimpeded by boundaries and blockages.

During our first month at the Maine house, I woke each day eager to see a cerulean sky reflected in water. As soon as morning light slipped into the windows, I jumped out of bed, pulled on some clothes, and grabbed binoculars to spy the seals and cormorants on distant rocks.

But all I saw was fog.

It was one of the foggiest Junes on record in Maine. Fog obliterated the horizon, enveloping shore and sky in endless opaque gray. Fog forms here when warm air over the land embraces colder air over the sea's Labrador Current, which travels all the way from the Arctic to chill our waters. So all I saw was fog.

Gone were the sightings recalled so fondly from previous visits:

Distant mountains looming behind a pebble-and-boulder-strewn beach.
Seagulls and plovers lined up on the flat rock close to shore.
A bald eagle alighting on a fir tree.

Seals lounging on rocky ledges.
Seaweed draping the rocks.
Loons diving.
The bay—
Gone.

All I could see was fog.

It was a deft disappearing act. It even made me doubt memories of these seascape emblems as the cold, dense fog imprisoned us most of the day for nearly a month. Despite being in a house with glass walls on three sides, there was nothing to see, and my spirit shrank with the vista. With peevishness in my voice, I complained to Frank, "We spent all this money on a view, and *all I see is fog!*"

But as we spent more time in Maine, I came to discover the blessings of sea smoke that reveals more by showing less.

Fog is especially prevalent on the Maine coast in autumn. One fall, my visiting photographer friend Lynn talks me into waking before sunrise so we can take pictures at dawn of Jordan Pond in Acadia National Park. Still half-asleep when the alarm goes off at 5:00 a.m., morning stupor unrelieved by coffee, I am somewhat resentful of not spending a leisurely morning at home. That resentment intensifies when it begins to get light out as we drive, and we are encapsulated in fog. *Great. We'll drive all that way to see nothing.*

Lynn is elated. "I hope it's still foggy when we get there," she says like a schoolkid on a field trip. As we climb and coast through the park, low-lying areas that hug the shore are filled with fog, but higher areas in the mountains have clear skies, so it is hard to predict what we will encounter at Jordan Pond. Lynn bemoans any signs of the fog lifting. I think she is being naive and doesn't realize how much mist can obliterate a decent view. But being the obliging host, I remain silent and continue to drive toward the pond. Upon arriving, we can hardly see the two rounded mountains, called the Bubbles, which flank Jordan pond. *So much for catching their reflections in the water, we can barely see the Bubbles against the sky.*

I'm about to suggest we try another spot in the park when Lynn jumps out of the car, whips out her camera and starts snapping pictures. With nothing else to do, I follow her, dragging my camera with me. But while framing shots, I realize how the blank backdrop of fog makes the fall colors of the brush in the meadow pop out. Drifts of scarlet huckleberry bushes in between amber shades of grasses and goldenrod become more striking when they don't have to compete with a blue sky. Soon I am snapping pictures as quickly as Lynn.

By the time we walk around the pond, the fog lifts somewhat, so we can see boulders breaking out of the water close to the shore, and the Bubbles twinned by their reflections in water. There is enough fog far off to soften the profile of these mountains in the distance and drape them with cottony drifts. Mist gives the Bubbles an aura of mystery and makes them contrast nicely with the boulders clearly highlighted in the foreground. Fog enhances many of the pictures like a spotlight illuminating a small sphere of scenery, while the rest disappears into darkness. It is akin to the chiaroscuro effect Rembrandt employed so well in his paintings that enables you to see what you wouldn't ordinarily notice.

The fog-induced spotlight continues on the drive back; it makes the stream in an estuary disappear into the mist and narrows the focus on the white froth of waves crashing against the cliffs, hiding the full extent of the ocean that powers them. Fog highlights trees in the foreground and then creates a subtle visual echo by lightening and softening the edges of the forest behind them. It also glistens the cranberries, turning them into rubies, and causes every twig to drip with sparkling diamonds of water.

I begin to see the value of fog.

Fog comes in many forms depending on when it appears and how thickly it paints the sky. Fog at sunrise can be gossamer with rays of sunlight glinting through it. By obliterating the separation of the sea from the distant horizon, fog creates a shimmering golden curtain that bedazzles. On other days fog comes in linear strands that weave in and out of the landscape, varying what they highlight, as if to say, *Look now before it disappears.*

One morning, fog stretches its way across the bay in a narrow band above which tops of trees float as if suspended in midair. Mesmerized, I watch as it comes in from a nearby point and then, in just a few minutes, makes its way down the bay, all the while staying in linear formation like a marching regiment. In seconds, this solid-seeming fog vanishes.

Another morning, the fog blends the sea seamlessly with the sky, erasing the horizon, leaving a vacuum of white mist bracketed by the aquas of water and sky. Seagulls space themselves evenly on their rocky perches, their reflected selves visible on the water, the fog surreally obscuring everything else. By the time I finish my coffee, the mist lifts and the mountains and houses across the bay return to my view, along with a cloudless sky. It is like waking up in the morning still caught in the haziness of dreams, then having the real world slowly come into focus.

Now fog is an opportunity.

When waking, I look out the window and hope it is foggy, so the four firs stretched out on the distant outcropping across the bay will be silhouetted by an ethereal silver mist. (And so that the nearby house and its ugly pier will vanish.)

I took my favorite photograph of our bay at high tide when it was encased in fog, revealing only the oblong triangle of trees on a nearby point, a line of black ducks before it. The fog paints the sky with soft striations of gray. Like a black-and-white photograph, the sea smoke pares down the scenery to an essential skeleton of visual meaning while softening all the edges like an impressionistic painting.

Fog is also an opportunity for the plants growing on the nutrient-deprived soils generated by the granite bedrock so prevalent in Down East Maine. Because its droplets are so much finer than raindrops and each droplet forms by condensing on nourishing dust specks, fog can carry as much as a thousand times more calcium, potassium, phosphorus, and other dissolved nutrients than rain. This enables a lushness of flora, from the towering conifers and the ghostly old man's beard lichen decorating their branches and swaying in the wind, to the blueberry bushes growing in the gaps between granite boulders covered with a brilliant array of lichen.

Fog also can feed the soul by providing a rejuvenating repose from the strenuous activities fostered by sunny days. On fair-weather days, stunning scenery draws me outside, like a childhood playmate knocking on the door and asking me to come out and explore. When the sun glints on the water, I'm compelled to bike to Acadia and see the sea plume against the rocks, kayak to the marshes to find yellowlegs and sandpipers, or walk to the estuary, picking blueberries along the way. But when it's foggy, I take a deep breath and expand inward, reminisce, and reflect—find the skeletal meaning within the cloak of flesh, the clarity in the confusion.

A foggy day can be the natural equivalent of the Sabbath—a day of rest and a time "to sense the grandeur of what is eternal in time," as the twentieth-century rabbi Abraham Joshua Heschel described this sacred day. He called it a "palace in time" and wrote that "the Sabbaths are our great cathedrals . . . sanctuaries that emerge from the magnificent stream of the year. . . . Six days a week we live under the tyranny of things of space; on the Sabbath we try to become attuned to holiness in time," in *The Sabbath: Its Meaning for Modern Man*.

As other rabbis have noted, the ancient Hebrew word for holy, *kadosh*, means separation, because when we separate ourselves from quotidian tasks—the busyness involved in making a living and a comfortable home—we can experience the vastness, the eternal, the greater sphere beyond our more grounded selfish concerns. We have to give ourselves empty time to find meaning. Empty time is also valuable for creativity. Neuroscience reveals that when our brain is on idle and not devoted to specific tasks, when we daydream and doodle in our mind, we can achieve new insights and make creative leaps.

I don't observe the Sabbath, but I do observe the emptiness of foggy days.

One recent misty morning triggered a memory of a similarly enshrouded day many years ago. On a rocky beach in Maine and only four or five years old, I was enjoying a sweet and chewy cooked mussel I had freshly plucked from its shell and plopped into my mouth. But then I bit down onto something crunchy. Disturbed by this unexpected sensation, I immediately spat out what I was eating. My mother noticed and asked me why I was making such a mess. When I told her about the strange crunch inside the mussel, she explained it was a pearl, and we sifted through what I had partially chewed to find a beautiful hard speck of iridescence.

Similarly, I spat out those foggy days with a great deal of distaste the first summer at our Maine house, but now I see what treasures they offer. When the mist hangs over the bay in an impenetrable curtain, I relish the time to sit quietly and inwardly process all I've seen or done recently. I try to journey beyond the surface and find, hidden in the delicious complexity of what I experience, a hard yet numinous essence that is timeless and inspires; a deeper strata of meaning. I mull over migrating butterflies, my need to name the birds, or the vastness of the night sky; I remember my brother intently gazing at the woods from his wheelchair, my father giving me the gift of a beating heart, and my mother moved by the rosy beauty of the sun sinking into the bay. What they signify becomes more palpable, substance gives rise to form, and glistening pearls suddenly appear—

Out of the fog.

CHAPTER EIGHT

Navigating Nature

With a storied history of getting lost, I never kayak to the marshes without Frank leading the way. But yearning to return to these wetlands filled with shorebirds one morning when Frank is gone and a glistening high tide beckons, I grab a pair of binoculars, encase myself in a kayak, and slip into our bay.

After maneuvering past rocks strewn with seaweed and paddling by lobster buoys striped in bright colors, I leave the narrow neck of water and enter a bigger expanse where three bays converge. Here the wind picks up, causing the sea to spray off the paddle.

You can find the marshes relatively easily by following the opposing rocky shore and its clinging conifers. Then turn left after spotting the large rock outcropping where sandpipers and plovers always stand at attention at high tide. From there, point your kayak toward the distant patch of chartreuse signaling sea grasses.

Following those directives and then entering the marsh, I remember to take the widest sinuous route. Alongside this liquid passageway through sedges, I'm delighted to discover yellowlegs probing their long beaks into the mud. But these wary birds aren't pleased to see me and fly away with their alarm call of three or four loud *tews* in succession. After the next bend in the waterway, a long-legged blue heron hunting for fish stretches its neck out and pauses before taking each step, like someone tiptoeing into the room of a sleeping baby. Eventually the watery opening in the marsh narrows, ending with the dark green backdrop of spruces and firs, so I turn around and backtrack out.

Now the hard part—finding the way back.

On the return ride, you have to enter the correct waterway after encountering where the three bays converge. This is difficult considering how similar the bays and their tree-lined shores are. Maine's coast is filled with fingerlike projections of land into the ocean with narrow stretches of water between them like I now face. Which finger is the one where my house lies? Is it the middle finger, the ring finger, or the pointer finger? Looking at each like a game show contestant asked to choose between three identical doors, I know that behind only one lies the prize.

If smart like some animals described in biologist Bernd Heinrich's book *The Homing Instinct*, I would use the position of the sun to help orient me. This orb in the sky serves as a compass for migrating butterflies, dragonflies, and many birds, including starlings, which travel in the right direction on sunny rather than cloudy days. Bees too rely on the sun to orient themselves. They return to their hives after feeding on flowers by heading back exactly the same way that they came, remembering which turns they took in relation to the sun.

But I am hopeless when it comes to remembering more than one turn and have no sense of direction. *Really.* Frank jokes that I turn the wrong way when exiting the bathroom in the middle of the night, and there's some truth to that; whenever leaving a building, I turn the opposite way I should to return home. And if you asked me to point to our closest town when in our house in Maine, I would have to guess.

This general ineptitude at navigating has fostered my amazement of how animals find their way across long distances, as featured in Heinrich's book. Consider the gull-like shearwater taken from its nest off the coast of Wales, flown to Boston encased in a crate, and released in Boston Harbor. This bird immediately headed east and flew across the Atlantic Ocean without using landmarks, returning to its home burrow a dozen days later. Sea turtles can also somehow find the same speck of land where they breed—a tiny island in the middle of the vast Atlantic —after spending two or three years in feeding grounds more than a thousand miles away.

But even birds that migrate over land astound. Their high-up, bird's-eye view might enable them to travel north using the edge of the coast to guide them, but how do they know when to fly lower to find the same plot of land they nested on a year ago, to find those nearby marshes I kayak through, to find our bay? Homing pigeons fitted with frosted contact lenses on their eyes still returned to their home lofts, despite being unable to see landmarks. How do monarch butterflies find those same forests in Mexico and salmon their ancestral spawning grounds? How does a mouse maneuver in the dark? What is it that I'm missing and they have?

Being directionally challenged is a family trait. My mother, her sister, and I all shared this trait. My aunt dealt with it by never going anywhere new on her own, thereby avoiding the stress of realizing she had no idea which way to turn to return home. My mother was more adventuresome, relying on maps. I tend to depend on landmarks, remembering what I passed to find the way back.

But landmarks are useful only if they are unique, I discover, after choosing a pathway out of the marsh. Quieting any preconceived notions of navigation failure, I opt for the middle finger of land and then search for the distant white granite boulder that edges our bay. Using it as a navigational beacon, I keep aiming for that boulder while paddling over water that has become choppy after leaving the marsh. Soon the wind blows stronger, whipping up whitecaps that occasionally splash into the kayak and make it more strenuous to maneuver. Assuming the uptick of wind and going against the current is why the return ride takes longer than the ride there, I keep paddling toward that white boulder on our bay, silencing the fear of being lost.

Someone once told me, "I don't mind getting lost because I've found the best places and had the best times meeting people when I've lost my way." But when I'm lost, panic ensues; I return to my four-year-old self who doesn't do a good job trailing after her mom in the department store and instead burrows into the tunnel underneath the dresses on a rack, traveling from one group of clothes to another until she emerges from a lineup of pants, looks around, and can't find her mom's black pumps and nylon-wrapped legs. Looking off to the distance in all directions, she can't even see her mother's green and pink paisley skirt, and her heart races with the thought that she is alone in the store with no one to look after her.

Why panic when lost? Is it the loss of control? But why is control necessary? Why not embrace whatever is encountered and see being lost as embarking on an adventure, exploring new territory? When my mother and brother died, wiping off major segments of the family map, two fingers out of four, a similar panic ensued; a feeling of being rudderless and not knowing where to turn next without the familiar landmarks of loved ones who always had been present.

The previous time I felt so discombobulated was after entering adolescence and having to assess who I was and how to fit in with others. Having spent a blissful childhood full of confidence, I felt unsure maneuvering through middle school, isolated by a nascent self-consciousness that amplified and reverberated any differences with fellow classmates. Then nature was comforting, especially the nature that Maine offered. Embraced by its towering trees that didn't judge, reassured by the eternal rhythm of its tides, and inspired by its night sky speckled with a multitude of stars, I melded into a vastness that shrank any concerns. So after tossing about, mourning one death in the family after another, like a kayak rocked by the wakes of other vessels passing, I came to Maine to discover a way out of this dark period.

But maybe that way requires getting lost.

Didn't explorers have to get lost in order to find someplace new? It would have been folly for them to know exactly where they were going. Wasn't it Christopher Columbus who thought he was in India when he first landed in America and hence called the natives Indians? And what did those brave explorers do after voyaging across oceans, battling scurvy, storms, and seasickness, let alone a lack of maps, when they encountered new worlds? They named those new places after what they left behind—New *York*, New *London*, New *Orleans*.

Even explorers must long for the familiar.

Perhaps we all feel the pull of the *familiar* and *family*, both words sharing the same domestic root, the same urge to nestle in our nests of origin. But when the death of your family uproots you, can it also be freeing, an opportunity to see the shape you assume when not molded by others?

From the moment he forged his way out of our mother's womb, my brother became the leader and I the follower, roles that barely faded in adulthood and were reinforced by gender stereotypes. When walking with Joe, I didn't bother noticing where I was going because I could always follow him. I envied how easily he remembered how to get from his Vermont house to my Pennsylvania home without having to refer to a map or directions. Once totally confused by the labyrinthine pathway we had to take in the hospital to reach my father's room, I asked Joe, "How do you remember where to go?" as he led the way, never wavering. "Oh, I just notice where we turned right and left," he said, as if it was natural to notate in his mind where he had been. That tendency to rely on Joe to lead the way also led to a pattern of not noticing where I was going and blithely following others throughout life.

But now that lack of paying attention is causing trouble.

Nearing the big white boulder I had been aiming my kayak toward, assuming it marked my home territory, I discover above it a huge house surrounded by a grassy lawn that looks nothing like my squat home nestled in the forest. That's when I realize that though I had oriented toward the boulder, it is the *wrong* boulder.

I am totally turned around.

It's as if someone had just removed the blindfold after being spun for Pin the Tail on the Donkey. Even though it is the middle of the day, I feel like I am experiencing night blindness, with the white boulder I had been using as a landmark wiped off my mental map and no other landmarks to guide me. *I have no idea where I am.* A surge of adrenaline revs up my heartbeat and tightens my back muscles as I stare at that house that isn't mine and long for something familiar.

If only I were a rat.

Rats and mice are notorious for finding their way through mazes or through houses in the dark, returning to the same entrance after scrounging for food. How do they do it? Norwegian researchers Edvard and May-Britt Moser set out to answer that question and ended up uncovering an intricate internal GPS in the brains of rodents. This specialized network of neurons continually updates and records information about the animal's speed, position, direction of movement, and distance from where it started. By mapping its pathway into memory, the neurons enable an animal to return to its starting location after traveling in unfamiliar territory and even to devise shortcuts. The types of neurons that comprise a rodent's inner GPS also are found in other mammals, including humans, and seem to explain the "dead reckoning" both animals and people (Joe?) can have of their place in space and which way to turn.

Studies suggest men rely on this internal GPS more than women when navigating, as they are more likely to track the turns they take, noting where they are in space when making their way in an unfamiliar area. Women, in contrast, are more likely to note where they are in relation to landmarks.

But landmarks are helpful only if they are the *correct* landmarks, and somehow the white boulder I had pointed my kayak toward had led me astray in the bay. After a few minutes of frantic scanning for other landmarks, I breathe deeper when there's something to recognize—Francis Point, the only point in our area devoid of houses. On previous kayak trips, I had admired its distinctive rounded granite blocks edging into water like the stone claws of a lion sculpture getting its toes wet. Seeing Francis Point meant I had gone too far, so I turn around and keep close to shore in order to recognize my house when it appears. On that *long* kayak ride back, there are white granite boulders about every thousand feet until I reach the one in our bay.

So much for *that* landmark.

While writing an article on the Mosers' research, I asked the charmingly modest yet Nobel prize–winning investigators if a faulty inner GPS could explain why I have no sense of direction. Edvard Moser responded that although there is probably a strong genetic component that determines our neuronal GPS, accurate navigation also depends on adequate memory and attention. "Quite often, people who say they don't find their way partly cannot do so because they don't pay attention to their surroundings. Like when I am engaged in conversation while following someone around in a new city, and I find myself totally lost afterward," Moser said.

Or like when blindly following Joe out of the house, I then can't remember how to find the way home without him.

Even without dead reckoning, darkness can be an asset rather than a handicap when finding one's way—something to welcome rather than to fear.

For millennia, mariners relied on the North Star in the northern hemisphere to serve as a guiding light when journeying vast distances by water with no landmarks in sight. These sailors calculated how many miles north they were from the equator by how high the North Star was from their horizon line, with stars of nearby constellations indicating how far east or west they had traveled. A long period of cloudy or foggy nights led some ships to stray way off course with deadly consequences, from running aground with hulls splintered by rocks, to sailors dying from scurvy, thirst, or starvation when ship supplies ran out after longer-than-planned-for journeys.

Some seafarers still rely on the stars to pilot their crafts, including Chadd Onohi Paishon, a master navigator with the Polynesian Voyaging Society. He steers canoes from Hawaii to Tahiti and beyond without any instruments, charts, or GPS, Malia Wollan reported in a *New York Times* article. She quoted Paishon as saying, "Stars are my friends." No wonder—without them, he would be lost at sea.

Harriet Tubman relied on the stars, especially the North Star, to guide her and others out of the darkness of slavery to freedom. Tubman was born a slave in 1822 in Maryland and used the Underground Railroad—a network of abolitionists who sheltered escaping slaves—to find freedom in Philadelphia in 1849. There she worked to pay for the supplies that enabled her to return to her home plantation where her brothers were still enslaved and lead them to freedom as well. Called "the Moses of her people," Tubman risked her life by returning thirteen different times so she could lead more than seventy family and friends out of slavery.

She was able to accomplish these freedom trips by traveling only at night when the cover of darkness protected slaves from bounty hunters. (During the day, she and those she shepherded hid in the marshes and woods Tubman knew so well.) The dark nights obliterated any landmarks, so Tubman was guided by the North Star in the "drinking gourd" the slaves called the Big Dipper. "I was conductor of the Underground Railroad for eight years and I never ran my train off the track and I never lost a passenger," Tubman said once at a gathering, her diminutive frame belying an inner strength. With the right guidance, she knew a venture in pitch-black darkness could be a road to freedom.

To avoid the danger of encountering predators, many birds also travel only at night, often over oceans, as they make their long migrations, biologist Bernd Heinrich notes. Just like Tubman, these birds orient themselves to the relatively stationary North Star and nearby constellations while in the northern hemisphere and to the Southern Cross constellation while in the southern hemisphere. (Other stars and constellations change their positions in the sky during the course of a night.) Birds raised in the laboratory without exposure to the nighttime sky are unable to orient. "Knowledge of the specific star patterns as such is thus not inherited, but the attention to them, the capacity to learn from them and respond to them is," Heinrich writes in *The Homing Instinct*.

Remarkably, warblers rely so strongly on star patterns to orient themselves that when researchers place them in a planetarium in which the starry backdrop has been rotated 180 degrees, they will reverse their flying direction and point north in the fall.

When traveling in the dark or when landmarks are missing, some animals also depend on magnetic patterns to point them in the right direction and show them where they are on the map. Our Earth has a magnetic core that creates magnetic field lines around it. Like the lines of a tight-fitting, vertically striped dress on the belly of a heavily pregnant woman, the lines of these force fields get stretched apart close to the equator on our planet. By sensing the magnetic force-field lines and their intensity and angle, some animals know which way they need to face to head north or south, as well as their approximate location on the globe as they traverse long distances.

There are also invisible force fields in a family that guide the actions of its members. Like magnetic poles, expectations are particularly powerful and can pull you forward or hold you back, especially if you internalize them, as I probably did when attending a large university nearly a thousand miles from home when only sixteen. Feeling like an adult after securing an apartment, I made my own meals, paid my own bills, and even found my own way to classes. But in some fashion, I still stayed the baby in the family. Seeking out older students as friends and a lover, I followed them in a way that had become instinctual since the first day I tottered after my brother.

I needed guidance.

Magnetic fields can be strong guides, but how do animals detect them? Scientists suspect that ability is linked to the iron-containing compounds called magnetite (lodestone) lodged in certain of their cells. This lodestone, like a compass needle, aligns to Earth's magnetic core akin to how iron filings line up in the same direction in response to a magnet. When crossing various magnetic force fields, the movement of this magnetite embedded in nerve cells could serve as a sensor for the magnetic patterns by which an animal navigates, triggering an electric signal in the animal's brain. Researchers have detected magnetite in the bellies of bees, the antennae of butterflies, the snouts of fish, the beaks and inner ears of birds, and even buried in human brains. Although they don't know for certain, scientists suspect this lodestone—which literally translates to "journey stone" and entered the English language when mariners began using lodestones as compasses—could put various animals in sway of forces in nature invisible to the human eye. There's also evidence that the visual system in some birds enables them to see the vertical magnetic force lines to which we are blind.

Other powerful yet invisible guides in much of the animal kingdom are the smells in an environment, although scents are less reliable beacons at a distance unless the wind or water consistently carries them without changing direction. Monarch butterflies migrating southward from Maine rely on the sun as a compass, as well as orienting themselves to magnetic fields. But some scientists speculate that the scent of the unique oyamel fir trees in western Mexico ultimately guides them to their highly specific winter destination. Salmon too are guided in part by smell when they have to leave the ocean and travel thousands of miles to return to ancestral spawning grounds in rivers and streams. Experiments show salmon will swim upstream only if that body of water has the particular blend of scents and flavors the young salmon were exposed to prior to migrating to the ocean.

Although it is not known exactly what drives salmon to make this arduous journey, scientists suspect the fish are motivated to return to where their predecessors found an environment suitable for generating their young. But sometimes salmon head home to spawn only to discover the unfamiliar—a dam that blocks their way, home waters that have become polluted or disrupted in their absence, an ancestral family that has disappeared.

M ost of my original family too has disappeared, leaving me to forge new territory in Maine, to be my own guide. Unable to rely on lodestones or an internal GPS for my journeys, I need to observe every detail, make note of those *unique* landmarks, and stop having a little-sister-tagalong mentality that leads to blindly following others without noticing the path taken. Surely I am capable of doing better. As a friend pointed out, "If you can notice the difference between the bird beak of a lesser and greater yellowlegs, you should be able to notice where you are going." I also need to stop panicking when lost and instead view being lost as a freeing adventure, an exploration of terra incognita.

Pay attention, I now tell myself when entering new territory, whether it's a bay with new nooks and crannies to explore or the new world where my mother and brother are missing.

CHAPTER NINE

Springtime

The forest is ominously silent—no love songs from flocks of robins, warblers, and thrushes that Frank and I usually hear during our summers in Maine. No buzzing bees. No droning mosquitos. Even the wind is silent with no tree leaves to rustle its song. But after we walk about a half mile, a creaky, quacky chorus of wood frogs breaks the silence. Where are these lusty amphibians and how can they muster the energy to chortle their ardor in this freezing weather?

We expected it to be warmer. It is the end of April, when spring is normally underway in Down East Maine, and we left behind in Philadelphia a colorful array of tulips in full bloom and trees sporting their bright new-leaf green hue. But after pulling into the driveway of our Maine house the previous night, we were discouraged to discover a patch of snow instead of daffodils. Over the nearly six-hundred-mile journey, we had gone back in time and reentered the black-and-white world of winter. Maybe we shouldn't have foregone spending our spring vacation in Philadelphia, I thought while zipping up my winter coat and lugging in wood to make a fire.

The sun tempts us outdoors the next day, but despite its warmth, I have to don a wool beret and gloves. We walk alongside the road and see that although nothing is blooming, the sphagnum moss has greened and fluffed out by soaking up the downpour of the prior day. Its chartreuse carpet glows beneath the dark stands of evergreens edging the road. Interspersed in this forest are occasional maple trees, but the buds of their branches haven't swelled and blushed red as they do just before their flowers burst out. There also are no catkins dangling from the white birches, which stand out like ghosts among the trunks of spruces and firs.

Yet the frogs must sense spring has sprung because they are croaking their mating calls. The combined snowmelt and recent massive rainfall have left a few pond-puddles in the ditches alongside the road. Could the frogs be there? Walking up to one of these one-foot-deep pools, we see ripples in the water, perhaps signaling the retreat of sunning amphibians. Peering into the rust-colored water lined with black maple leaves, we are excited to see something moving within it. But this animal isn't quickly burying itself deeper into the muck, leaving behind a cloud in the water like a frog would upon discovery. Instead its long narrow body slowly undulates. It is so close to us we can make out its ribs underneath smooth stretched skin. It has two small legs on either side of its body, and a long tail that propels it. Slapped onto its back like stickers are perfectly round bright yellow spots that look surreal compared to the dull dark gray background of its body. The creature keeps diving to the bottom of the pool and then swimming up to a shimmering jellylike mass floating on the surface, tinged with green, and dotted with black eggs.

What could it be? Returning home, I search the internet and discover that while looking for frogs, we had inadvertently discovered a yellow-spotted salamander. You rarely get to glimpse this elusive nocturnal amphibian, which normally hides in the forest underneath leaf litter or in burrows. But at this time of year, snowmelt and spring downpours leave behind temporary ponds called vernal pools that serve as salamander breeding grounds. These animals prefer to lay their eggs in the pools so they are free from predation of fish inhabiting larger ponds. The fertilized eggs hatch into tadpoles that a few months later sprout legs just in time to walk out of the shallow water before it dries up in the summer heat.

The unexpected discovery of the salamander reminds me of when, years ago, Frank and I went on a quest to discover the spring peepers in Maryland that were filling the air with their love songs. To attract mates, males of these frogs have a vocal sac they expand and deflate to make loud high-pitched peeps similar to but louder than the insistent peeping of chicks. The chorus of spring peepers was so resounding during early evenings in spring, we were determined to see these animals we had only heard. Walking through a small patch of woods to a nearby pond, the wavering beams of our flashlights revealed snippets of scenery along the way: a tangle of vines around a tree trunk, brush giving way to meadow. The seductive perfume of the tree flowers suffused the evening air that was starting to lose the chill of winter. Sitting among the tall grasses fringing the pond, which seemed to be the epicenter of the continual peeping, we focused our flashlight beams on the water.

But we were frustrated after several minutes when no frog appeared in our sights. *How could something that loud and close not be seen?* Eventually we gave up, turned off our flashlights, and just sat and listened, enjoying the pulsating sound that seemed to come from all around us and merge with our heartbeats, connecting us to one of nature's rhythms. As we stood to leave, I turned my flashlight on. When it was still pointed at the ground, its light revealed a delightful surprise—on almost every stalk of grass clung a tiny frog belting his heart out! We didn't expect frogs so loud could be so small—less than an inch long—and that was why we missed seeing the spring peepers when we began our search.

What other things do we miss in nature—and in ourselves and others—by having the shape of what we perceive already chiseled by what we expect? How often do heavily laden assumptions prevent the childlike surprise and wonder induced by something unforeseen? There is a two-sidedness to the experience we accumulate with age. Although it enables us to better handle the expected, it can blind us to the unexpected. Coming to Maine expecting to see the usual signs of spring, I would have missed a key indicator that the vernal transition was already underway if it hadn't been for the croaking of frogs that prompted a look into a roadside ditch where I spotted the salamander.

Floating masses of salamander eggs signal the beginning of spring in New England for those attentive to them. In orgies that outdo the renowned bacchanal gatherings of the ancient Romans, yellow-spotted salamanders are particularly known for their mating rain dances that roil the waters of vernal pools. During these nighttime nuptials, males squirt out their sperm, which sinks to the bottom of the oversized puddles. The next day, females lay their eggs in floating gelatinous masses and then dredge up sperm from the bottom of the pools to fertilize them, renewing the endless cycle of life. If mating occurs too late in the spring, there won't be enough time for the salamander tadpoles to mature and sprout legs before the ponds dry up.

Timing is everything in nature, and I am thrilled to have come at just the right time to see the yellow-spotted salamander doing her part to carry out her species' continuity. I no longer bemoan the wintry weather, pine for the spring flowers we left behind, nor express disappointment at what we encounter in Maine. The tulips will still be there when I return to Philly, and I treasure our unexpected sighting of the salamander, astonished that even a mere roadside ditch filled with snow-melt and rainwater can be a vital nursery for new life—as long as the salamander times it right.

CHAPTER TEN

They Say There Are Moose

Heat silences the squawking of the seagulls, and the red squirrels don't even have the energy to scold in the unusual 90-degree weather. The bay can't muster a breeze and lies stagnant. It is so hot I can't move, can't think, can't work. Not until high tide, when I can wade into the water and have its blessedly frigid Labrador Current wash away any memory of warmth.

Surrounded by the silent forest and bay, there is an emptiness accentuated by being alone at the house this week, Frank and our daughter Eva having returned to Philly. Where has all the wildlife gone? There's not even a porcupine, which often lounges during the day in the high branches of the maple tree, its arms dangling languidly. How do they cool off—the porcupine, the deer, the hummingbirds that work so hard to stay aloft, the moose with its shaggy coat that must be roasting in this heat? Where *are* they?

It feels like I am the last living soul left on a seared planet.

Finding it too hot to work, I read about moose instead. On extremely hot days, moose seek refuge by soaking in cool shallow water, the biologist Valerius Geist writes in his book *Moose*. They are excellent swimmers that will venture far in the ocean—so far that killer whales have been known to attack them. Moose actually seem to have a love affair with water. Like small children, they'll rear up and then splash puddles and pounce on each ocean wave as it breaks on shore. And like sensual adults, they also enjoy soaking in hot springs on cold days. The moose's nose has self-sealing nostrils so it can feed underwater without having to raise its head with every bite like a deer. Aquatic plants are one of the moose's favored foods. Geist's book is filled with pictures of moose in lakes and oceans with water streaming from their wide noses like mini waterfalls and reeds dangling from their muzzles.

They say there are moose in our woods, but I've never seen one. That's because they are so good at camouflaging themselves, say Rosemary and Garry, our friends who run the local art gallery. Despite their big obtrusive antlers, long skinny legs, and thousand-pound bodies so large they look like they just walked in from the Pleistocene, the moose blend into the background, and you don't even know they are there. Garry said that one morning, while looking out his kitchen window, he spotted a moose on the edge of his yard by the forest. Wanting to capture the moose with a picture, Garry went to get his camera in another room. But when he returned and tried focusing the camera on where he last saw the animal, he couldn't find the moose. It wasn't until after his dog chased it away that he realized the moose was still in the same spot. But because it had been motionless, its features fused with that of the forest. As another friend described her moose sighting, "I was driving and I noticed that the trees on the side of the road were suddenly walking in front of my car."

During the several summers we've been up in Maine, I've seen lots of wildlife. Foxes that flash their auburn tails as they leap across the road. Porcupines ambling slowly into the yard, their impish pitch-black faces edged with white-tipped quills. Nuthatches, woodpeckers, and warblers that fill the trees, while loons, eiders, and cormorants splash in the bay.

But no moose. *How can something so big be so hard to find?*

Not able to find them in the forest, I find moose in Geist's book. Reading about these animals, I am flabbergasted. *I had no idea.* Consider how they court each other: as part of the mating game, the bull grows (in just four or five months!) those giant antlers that can spread to seven feet and weigh as much as thirty-five pounds. The bull uses his antlers to fend off other males that want to mate, so the bigger they are, the more likely a bull gets his cow. But the *cow* isn't attracted to the one with the biggest antlers. What gets a cow moose excited isn't the sight of a big brawny bull strutting into her territory or the sound of him bellowing. No, the cow is enticed by something far more subtle, seductive, and salacious—the bull's urine. Part of the reason why moose have those enormous noses is because they give them a superlative sense of smell, and the smell of pee just drives cows wild with desire. While the bull urinates, they run circles around him, fighting each other to be the first to wallow in the pungent soaked ground he leaves after relieving himself. Somehow the urine bonds that lucky pee-soaked cow to the moose, and she follows her nose, which means she follows *him* because, just after peeing, he smacks the pool of urine while leaning over it so it splashes onto his antlers and the mound of flesh that hangs below his chin. Called a bell, this shaggy protuberance acts like a scent dispenser. That's what makes the moose *really* attractive to the cow. Pee.

Scientists suspect the scent of the bull's urine stirs up a cow's hormones, making her fertile. But *cow* urine also has an important part to play in moose sex. A bull can detect if a cow is ready to have sex and be impregnated by sampling her urine. And how does he do this sampling? By having the cow pee on him. Although it seems kinky, after he licks the cow's vulva, the cow pees on the bull, who makes sure her urine trickles over his nose. Then the bull curls back his upper lip, exposing his palate, and goes into a kind of swoon, slowly moving his head to and fro entranced. Though it looks like he's leering in ecstasy, this bizarre behavior lets him detect how sexually receptive the cow will be—the urine slips between a small cleft in his palate leading to a special sensory organ that can detect key hormones. Foreplay? *I had no idea.*

All this reading about moose has made me *really* want to see one, but even moose biologists can have a hard time spotting these animals in the wild because they can be extremely skittish when they detect humans in their midst. Some moose are so wary that they only emerge from the forest at night in areas populated by people. These animals have an amazing ability to hear even tiny sounds due to their large palmate antlers, which enable echolocation. Once when Geist was stalking a moose, he realized the rustling noises made by his clothes were alerting it to his presence and causing the moose to leave whenever he got close. So he stripped and followed the moose barefoot. There's something endearing about the image of a naked and barefoot biologist acting like a wood sprite, hiding behind trees as he trails the moose with its heavy coat of fur and hard hooves.

One thing you don't want to do is surprise a moose, because it may respond by attacking you with its barbed antlers or the powerful kicks of its legs. The hooves of a moose are large and its big bones dense and heavy, so one kick can kill.

Despite their elusiveness, Joe occasionally would see moose in the Vermont countryside where he lived. He once told me that shortly after he was diagnosed with ALS, he was driving by a misty field when he noticed that the field had a visitor—an enormous bull moose, his large antlers stretching out from either side of his head like bony serrated wings. Wanting to capture the moose with his camera, my brother stopped his car and got out. Then Joe weighed his curiosity and urge to go closer to the animal with his usual caution. He couldn't help but be aware that a big animal carrying such an impressive hard-edged rack could easily harm, if not kill, a slender human with nothing but a few soft hairs on top of his balding head.

As he related the incident later, Joe crouched low to the ground for a few seconds, debating whether to narrow the distance between him and the majestic moose. That's when his fatal ALS diagnosis for once proved worthwhile. *What do I have to lose?* he thought to himself and crept so close to the animal that the moose's profile filled his photo's frame.

It's too hot a day to be out stalking moose, although stripping down is not such a bad idea. The incongruity of Maine being hot makes the searing temperatures all the more surreal. Normally we're blessed with perfect summer days with temperatures in the upper 70s or lower 80s this far north. Such comfortable conditions explain why, in the era before air conditioning, East Coasters who could afford it migrated up to Maine in the summer along with the warblers. There's even an old established colony of Philadelphians on a portion of our peninsula that the locals call "Philadelphia-on-the-Rocks."

But today there's no escaping the scorching temperatures. I try to write, but no words come from my fried brain, and any impulse to be productive has melted. Feeling myself wilt, I wait for high tide to water the empty, parched bay. The heat has blackened its amber rockweed and kelp, caked the mud with a gray pallor, and dulled the normally spring-green reeds.

Finally, when two black-bellied plovers tenaciously cling to the last remaining rock in the bay still above water, I fling off my clothes and slip into a swimsuit. Gingerly walking over seaweed and slippery rock, each step takes me deeper into the icy water, causing gasps of shock. But after taking the plunge and submerging my overheated head in the bay, I come alive again, like the seaweed that dances when the water returns at high tide. Every skin cell tingles as it awakens, and there's this exhilarating relief as my overheated body gets cooled by the 60-degree water and I become one with a more benevolent Mother Nature.

A surge of energy propels me to swim to my neighbor's cabin and back. Then floating effortlessly in the sparkling salt water, I welcome the sun's rays I previously had shunned. Thoughts drift away with the water, any discomforts and concerns no longer present as I merge with the ocean.

Refreshed, I head to the shower. Though not bothering to turn on any hot water, the cold splash feels warm as I wash off the salt. The air is deadly still and quiet, and the heat and humidity weighty as I eat dinner and watch the hazy sky ripen into warm tones. It is also sweltering later when numerous stars speckle the sky with their milky dust.

I strip down and slip into bed without even a sheet for cover. About to drift into slumber, I jolt upright when I hear a tremendous splashing in the water followed by loud snorting. The snort is louder than that of a deer, and the splash is certainly bigger than something that could come from a deer or waterfowl. Bear are here, but they don't snort, nor would coyote or fox, and a bobcat would never get into the water. Too tired to pull myself out of bed, find a flashlight, and walk down to the bay to investigate, I start to wind down again when I realize what I've probably just heard.

A moose.

Still unseen but maybe heard at last. While entering that hazy zone between wakefulness and sleep, where all self-consciousness disappears, I feel both the comfort and thrill of possibly sharing the same patch of salt water with a magnificent moose. Maybe the animal, like I, just needed to cool off and probably soon will be snoring nearby. Falling asleep, I find my dreams splashed with images of this splendid elusive creature who comes closer the deeper I slip into slumber until it is near enough to nuzzle my face in its bell and embrace its enormous muzzle. A quest fulfilled—if only in a dream.

CHAPTER ELEVEN

Winter

Something vital is missing.

The bay is eerily silent—no birds calling, no seals growling. Broken upturned sheets of ice piled on one another give the shore a ruffled appearance. Breath plumes upward in the near-zero-temperature air, and the cold nips at any exposed skin. Looking through the binoculars, I scan the water for the usual waterfowl but find only a few eider and bufflehead ducks in their winter black-and-white attire. There are no signs of the chipmunk that last summer scurried over our feet to climb into Jake's discarded bowl on the ground, licking its oatmeal remnants while we looked on with amusement. Nor is there any evidence of the brown-and-white weasel that, like the nursery rhyme, once surprised me by popping out of a small burrow next to my feet, raising its sleek body to rest on its hind legs, and staring at me with its teddy bear–like face before scampering off. There's no noisy chatter of chickadees, nasal honkings of nuthatches, nor can I see the tiny kinglets that were flitting about like moths in the spruces before we left last November, even though my bird book claims all of these birds are year-round residents up here. Particularly striking is the absence of the usually omnipresent squawking of gulls.

The bay is barren.

We didn't know what to expect when Frank and I, and Eva home from college with boyfriend in tow, deciding to experience winter in Maine, arrived the previous night after a storm freshly dumped two feet of snow. As we drove down our driveway, sparkling, snow-laden limbs of spruces and firs reached out to welcome us, while the brush lay hidden under a continuous thick white blanket. Clumps of smaller saplings completely encased by snow looked like children pretending to be ghosts by hiding under white sheets.

The scene is otherworldly, as if we had just passed through the magic closet into the frozen world of Narnia. To complete the picture of this make-believe land, the lamppost at the end of our driveway is topped by a peaked cap of snow. By dropping just a few degrees in temperature, water had completely morphed the forms it encountered, like the Ice Queen in Narnia, who changed everyone she touched into frozen statues. But unlike the frigid queen, the freezing temperatures do us no harm and instead cause everything to blossom with beauty, as snow glistening from the car headlights outlines each branch on every tree. The next morning, the sun paints the snow with glitter, and icicles glint from the eaves of the roof. But the more I venture out in the freezing temperatures, the more I am puzzled by what is not there.

Animals.

Where have all the animals gone? Is Maine just a summer vacationland for them too? If not, how do they survive the cold temperatures and snow?

The two main threats to an animal's life during subfreezing—and especially subzero temperatures—are starving and freezing to death, I discover after reading biologist Bernd Heinrich's book *Winter World*. But it's a cruel catch-22 that the main strategy mammals can use to prevent themselves from freezing to death makes them more likely to starve to death, and the main trick they can use to avoid starvation makes them more likely to freeze. The end result? A delicate dance to sidestep death.

Let me explain. Mammals have a great ability to warm themselves via heat given off by their shivering, and some birds, such as chickadees, also survive cold winter nights by shivering in their sleep. But you need a lot of calories to shiver for long periods, which is a problem given that food is scarce during winter months, when fall berries are long gone, most insects are hibernating, and many large animals' prey, such as mice and chipmunks, keep to their burrows for long stretches of time to avoid the cold.

A way to avoid starvation when food is scarce is to slow the metabolic engine that keeps the body running so that it requires less fuel.

This winter survival strategy is akin to what saves the ice skater who falls through the ice of a pond or lake, and lies under water not breathing until she is rescued ten minutes later. Unresponsive and seemingly dead at first, she miraculously sputters back to life without major problems even though most people become brain-dead if they are deprived of oxygen for just four minutes. But fortunately for the ice skater, the frigid water slowed her metabolism so she needs much less oxygen and can survive longer without it. Such slowed-down metabolism is called torpor.

Some animals, such as bears, become torpid for most of the winter so they rarely have to eat and instead fall into the deep dreamless sleep of hibernation. Other animals, such as chipmunks, store seeds in their underground burrows to limit the amount of time they have to spend torpid. But the trick to becoming torpid is not to let the body temperature fall too low, so that the animal can still be nominally functional and revive itself when temperatures rise or, alternatively, can rev itself up with emergency shivering or foraging and feeding when temperatures fall too low. Torpid animals can fall in death's clutches if predators discover them. A torpid chipmunk has no chance of escaping a weasel that ventures into its burrow.

Another winter survival strategy that anyone who beds with a spouse, dog, or cat knows is to huddle together. Mice, birds, and honeybees use this tactic to stay warm. Animals also can build themselves insulating nests or burrows or temporarily borrow them. Weasels don't build permanent dens or nests because they can make their way into those of the rodents they kill, resting in their warm and cozy abodes after ungratefully eating their hosts.

Of course, the most obvious strategy for staying warm in winter is to follow the Scandinavian motto, "There's no such thing as bad weather, just bad clothing." The paragon of an animal clothed well for winter is the mink, which has as many as 44,000 hairs per square inch of pelt, compared to a paltry 350 hairs per square inch on the human head, Heinrich notes. Many animals, such as foxes and red squirrels, grow a thicker coat of fur for winter. Winter birds like chickadees have denser feathers they can fluff out for further insulation. The eiderdown feathers that fill my winter coat were originally grown to protect the ducks from the cold.

Eiderdown is probably what also saved a group of us years ago when we decided to combine a cross-country ski trip in Wisconsin with winter camping. We prepared for the cold at night by mummifying ourselves into two down sleeping bags apiece. We thought the temperature would hover around zero, not the *twenty below zero* temperature we actually experienced. The next morning, waking up to a cold and wet sensation on my face, I saw snow falling *inside* our tent: our breath freezing once it hit the domed enclosure was then drifting back down as ice crystals. But the eiderdown in our sleeping bags kept us warm.

You'd think that birds, who are such fabulous nest makers, would excel at making warm winter abodes. For example, in the spring, after the kinglet weaves together strands of spiderwebs, caterpillar silk, moss, lichen, paper birch bark, and twigs to make her cup nest, she then lines it with rabbit down and thousands of bird feathers to help ensure her clutches stay warm. But as Heinrich noted, the kinglets, like most birds, abandon these cozy spring nests well before winter, even if they continue to reside in the same area, for reasons not completely understood. Admittedly, such a beautifully constructed open-cup nest of the kinglet would not be practical in winter because it would fill with snow, Heinrich pointed out, but the birds could have evolved like other birds to construct domed nests that would prevent the snow from entering.

This puzzled Heinrich—how can a tiny bird like a kinglet, which weighs no more than a few coins and is the size of a golf ball, possibly keep itself warm without a nest when temperatures plunge into the double digits below zero? Kinglets are so miniscule and fast that most people never see them as they dart in and out of bushes and tree branches. But I have a certain fondness for these birds because, unfortunately for them, they frequently fly into the reflective windows of my house, ending up temporarily stunned and immobile on the deck floor. I once held a stunned kinglet in my palm until it recovered enough to fly away to safety. It was a little round bundle of fluff, a drab olive and gray color except for a brilliant patch of yellow (the kinglet's crown) on the top of its tiny head. But is the kinglet that once graced my palm safe now that everything is frigid and frozen? And what about nuthatches, chickadees, and other winter birds we enjoy seeing? Are they finding enough food and going to be around to greet us come spring? Even though there's no sight or sound of these birds, I have a sense that they are there somewhere and hope they are tucked away in some sheltered place relatively warm and free from harm.

Ironically, the one place that provides signs of wildlife is somewhere that had been seemingly devoid of it during summer. That's because, with the right equipment, the snow enhances our ability to explore new places, including a nearby opening in the forest that had always intrigued me in warmer weather but was inaccessible due to its boggy nature. Now that this heath is frozen over, we can venture into it. Our neighbor Joe kindly lends us two pairs of cross-country skis, and Frank and I follow his lead and ski on top of the frozen stream in the heath, a pathway into new territory.

Sailing through the snow, the cold is at first a shocking slap in the face, but it isn't long before we warm up and start shedding our jackets. We ski close to long-dead trees whose skeletal remains could be spied only at a distance in the warmer months. A few lichen-mottled boulders line the edge of the bog, the snow outlining their cracks. Dark stalks from last fall's vegetation poke out of the crystalline blanket in scattered clumps, offering filigreed silhouettes against a white background. The stark contrasts dazzle, especially with the snow glittering in the sun. The scene has the elegance of a formal affair, a rare celebration with everyone dressed in black and white and diamonds sparkling everywhere.

A vigilant scan of the horizon for signs of animals proves fruitless, so I turn my gaze downward to look for animal tracks in the snow, searching for the broken heart–shaped indentations of deer, rabbits' teardrop-shaped imprints, and the doglike prints of fox. Tales can be told from tracks left in snow, as Aldo Leopold pointed out in his book *Sand County Almanac*. He discerned a skirmish between a rabbit and an owl and even divined the winner from clues in the pattern of tracks he saw. Once, years ago when Frank and I went for a walk in the woods in Maryland after a major snowfall, we glimpsed the waving orange tail of a fox further down the trail. To catch up with it and get a better sighting, we followed its tracks in the snow. Eventually we lost it before completing the loop through the forest and never saw the fox again. But looking behind us, we were surprised to see fox tracks nearby. Apparently, we weren't following the fox, the fox was following us!

It's not likely we will see a fox or its tracks today because these animals don't like to expend effort wallowing through deep, fluffy snow. Instead they curl up and wrap their fluffy tails around them to keep warm, staying inactive for a few days until hares, squirrels, and deer have packed down some trails. We are probably doing the foxes a favor with our skis, providing them a future path.

It isn't until we swoosh through the snow for about an hour that I finally spot a small set of tracks. Bending down to examine one of the snow prints, I see a series of roundish blobs with four smaller indentations above each. Who could have made those? Looking closer, I realize the prints are a giant version of a cat's paw prints and then it hits me which animal most likely left them—a *bobcat!*

Neighbors had told me they had seen bobcats on our peninsula, but I had never spotted these animals, which resemble tabby cats but are about twice as big and have more black spots than stripes on their tawny coats. Bobcats also have furrier jowls and telltale black pointed tufts of hair on the tips of their ears. Their namesake is explained by their short (bobbed) tails, as well as by their distinctive bobbing gait due to larger and more muscular hind legs.

But bobcats are close enough in appearance to domestic cats that one woman driving in rural Maine at night put one in her car after she accidentally struck it unconscious while driving. The bobcat woke up about ten minutes later when she entered Bangor. Realizing at that point that she didn't have an injured pet needing a veterinarian in her car, but rather an extremely unhappy wild animal, she immediately pulled over and jumped out. The bobcat did the same while her car door was open.

The bobcat tracks I see on the frozen stream don't lead me to a sighting of the animal, but this sign that we are not alone in the white wilderness is heartening.

I keep thinking about the kinglets, which play a starring role in Heinrich's book on how animals survive the winter. These birds normally dine on insects they glean from twigs. But what insects could they find in the middle of winter, and how could they find enough of them to eat three times their body weight each short winter day in order to stay warm? As Heinrich noted, if kinglets are without food for only an hour or two during the day, they could starve and freeze to death. Intrigued by this conundrum, Heinrich investigated wild kinglets in Maine in winter and discovered a surprise—buried in their gizzards were newly swallowed inchworms. Who would have thought these insects were around when the temperature plunges below freezing, but when Heinrich vigorously shook some branches of trees, a shower of these frozen caterpillars fell to the snow below. The inchworms were the larvae of moths that overwinter on the twigs of various trees—frozen lifelines for famished kinglets.

Heinrich solved one piece of the puzzle—what kinglets eat in winter. But even on a good foraging day, such food could not provide enough calories for the birds to shiver their way through a long winter's night when temperatures are far below zero, he calculated, even if they became torpid, unless these birds have something else protecting them from the cold.

Shelter.

After skiing awhile, I stop searching for tracks on top of the snow and instead try to imagine animal life that might be hiding and sheltered *within* the snow. Heinrich pointed out that when temperatures dip below freezing, the insulating snowpack provides a warmer haven where birds, mice, and voles create intricate networks of tunnels and nests in the snow. These winter retreats are hidden from the sight of their predators, who must rely on a combination of acute hearing and quick lunges to catch them. Fox hearing is especially attuned to the lower frequencies made by small animals scuttling in snow or underbrush. One biologist watched as a fox sitting motionless in a snowy field suddenly dived into the snow, nabbing a mouse two feet below the surface. It's astonishing that flying owls can hear the scurrying of voles in snow cover as far as one hundred feet away from them. After making a split-second descent, this raptor uses its long sharp talons to yank a vole out of its icy abode and into its warm gullet.

The voles may make their homes in snowy burrows during the winter, but what kind of home protects the kinglet? It is too small and frail to dig under the snow like a grouse. Birds that use snow as shelter must be strong enough to poke through the ice that crusts these frozen dwellings when sunlight warms and melts their surface and later cold temperatures refreeze it into an icy armor, Heinrich noted. Knowing kinglets abandon their nests after raising their young and stumped about where they shelter in winter, he persistently tracked kinglets he saw in a Maine forest until dusk, hoping to glimpse where they spent the night, but was unsuccessful at this task. Then a graduate student of his, while walking before sunrise in the forest, accidentally flushed out a pair of kinglets from a brush pile on the ground. The brush pile was covered with a heavy layer of insulating snow. Heinrich surmised that kinglets must use these and other impromptu shelters found at the end of the day when they can no longer forage. These birds don't waste precious calories flying back to individual nests and instead forage in groups and then keep themselves from freezing to death by huddling through the night together in snow-covered havens.

But Heinrich noted that even with such shelters, kinglets still live on the razor-sharp edge of life and death during winter, with only about one out of ten nestlings surviving winter each year. Consequently, kinglets compensate by raising unusually large numbers of young in early spring and summer. Most songbirds in New England lay four to five eggs per clutch, but kinglets lay twice as many. It's also not unusual for a mated pair of kinglets to tend to two nests and clutches simultaneously, the female building a new nest in which she lays more eggs after the previous clutch no longer needs her body warmth and can be tended by the male. More than three-quarters of the eggs laid become fully-fledged kinglets, a nesting success exceptionally high for any bird.

Kinglets are the animal equivalent of annual plants, Heinrich concluded. Unlike perennial plants, which survive the winter in an underground state of dormancy and then send up shoots in spring, annual plants die in winter but produce so many seeds before dying that enough survive to sprout in spring. Similarly, kinglets rely on their large number of eggs and excellent tending of their young to provide the next crop of kinglets, few of which survive the bitter cold winter.

This may seem a heartless strategy for survival, and if the kinglets have some sort of sentience, I suppose they might be disturbed by how their efforts at diligent parenting result in such a paltry number of their young living until next spring. Do the ends justify the means? I cannot answer that question for the kinglet. I can only be grateful that next summer I will see their small nimble forms flitting about my yard, stalwart survivors of a challenging season.

Unlike the brush piles blanketed with snow that kinglets use for shelter, beaver lodges offer more protection and warmth. We ski past a few of these large snow-covered humps of brush above the frozen stream. Beavers make these conical huts out of sticks and mud, whose cement-hard walls are about a foot thick and can extend six feet high. These lodges provide both insulation from the cold and protection from predators. As we ski past them, I imagine the beaver families huddling inside, breathing through a vent hole covered by a latticework of sticks. Given that as many as a dozen beavers may be present inside a dam, it can be a tight squeeze.

Beavers don't hibernate. Their collective warmth and frequent underwater foraging trips to nearby stashes of branches enable them to survive the winter. Beavers can dine on wood because they harbor cellulose-digesting bacteria in their guts. To acquire even more calories from their sparse winter diets, they eat their own feces. Beavers also rely on body fat built up during the fall, and they drop their body temperatures slightly in winter so they have to make only a trip a day in the ice-cold water to feed.

After skiing around the snow-encased beaver lodges, I am ready to retreat to my own snow-topped lodge, eager to be in front of a warm fire, thawing numb fingers by wrapping them around a steaming fragrant mug of chai tea. Peeling off wet clothes once we get there and slipping into cuddly fleece, my legs and feet start to tingle as they warm up—a feeling that brings back childhood memories of frozen extremities coming back to life after hours spent building snow forts.

We gather around the fire and play a rousing round of the board game Settlers. I am thankful for our winter sojourn that is corralling my daughter and her boyfriend indoors that night with us. If we were back home in Philly, there would have been sparse sightings of these two, as they would be busy spending their evenings traversing city streets with friends. But here in the middle of the silent frozen forest, the heat of the fire draws us close together like a family of beavers huddled in their huts. Humans are the only animals known to make fires, Heinrich pointed out, which certainly abetted our winter survival early in our evolution.

Frank stirs the embers and adds another log to the woodstove while I watch its flames, soaking up its radiant warmth that is like the hot sun on a summer's day. How appropriate, I think, realizing the warmth emanating from the fire is the stored-up sunlight in logs that once were trees. I'm thankful for this gift from both the forest and our Ice Age ancestors, because otherwise instead of being cozy and comfortable, we might have spent the night shivering like the chickadee or torpid like the kinglet in a sleep devoid of dreams from which we just might not awaken.

PART THREE

Losses and Life Cycles

Behind the thing seen must lie the greater thing unseen.

—Freeman Tilden, *The Fifth Essence*

CHAPTER TWELVE

Tugged by the Tides

You go about your business, whatever it may be, with no thought to the sea. But always at the back of your consciousness you know what it is doing. In the middle of a conversation or waking in the dead of night you know without looking "the tide has just turned" or "the wind has shifted and she's started to pile up on Western Island." The sea has become a part of you, just as the beating of your heart and the rhythm of your breathing are parts of you.

—Louise Dickinson Rich, *The Peninsula*

Eventually tides will be the only calendar you believe in.

—Mary Oliver, *Evidence*

Everything in the universe is constantly changing, and nothing stays the same, and we must understand how quickly time flows by if we are to wake up and truly live our lives.

—Ruth Ozeki, *A Tale for the Time Being*

When Jake was three and the whole world revolved around him, he thought the moon did too. Once he pointed a finger on his dimpled hand up to the sky, where the moon and a few stars appeared within the rosy afterglow of sunset. "Look! My moon is following me!" he said, flashing his baby teeth–smile, blue eyes sparkling. From Jake's small perspective, no matter where he went at night, the moon did too. With the persistence of a loyal dog, the moon followed him home from his friend Justin's house, beamed above when he rode his tricycle back from our local restaurant, and shined in the window above his bed when he went to sleep. He could count on that.

But of course as he grew older, Jake realized the moon was not following him, and its nighttime glow faded from his consciousness. The colorful flashing neon lights of New York and other cities he's lived in as an adult mesmerized him more than the white orb high in the sky. After years spent living in cities, I too took the moon for granted, barely aware of its comings and goings and certainly not compelled by them. But that all changed when Frank and I started spending our summers in Maine by the bay.

That's when I became a follower of the moon.

The powerful pull of the moon is especially apparent on the Maine shore, where it creates thirteen-foot tides that routinely fill and empty bays and determine daily rhythms of activity. On my cobbled U-shaped bay, the underwater real estate opens up twice each day, revealing denizens with just a few hours to make the most of their temporary stay on land. Some scurry about like tourists released from a cruise ship. One adventuresome crab, venturing sideways as far as the ledge that abuts the bay, was surprised to encounter a landlubber in an Adirondack chair. Snails hunker down in their shells or roam in tidal pools where they are shielded from the dry air until the sea washes them again.

Snails and crabs aren't the only ones exposed by the tug of the moon at low tide. It also creates ephemeral pathways to teardrop islands in the distant sea. At a local beach at high tide, a wide swath of ocean separates you from one of these tiny islands, which beckons with its outcroppings topped with the jagged jades of conifers. But if you are fortunate to be there close to low tide, within minutes a triangle of pebbles, periwinkles, and cobbles suddenly appears next to the linear shore and points to the distant island. Like Moses's parting of the Red Sea, this arrow of emerging land quickly spreads wider and longer until it forms a crunchy barnacle-lined passageway to the previously inaccessible Bar Island. At this point and no later, you must walk this bridge of stones to explore the island because after a mere hour, the sea will seep in and surround it again.

If deaf to the ticking of the tidal clock, I miss the limited time there is to climb Bar Island's basalt boulders, which resemble beached whales, and admire its driftwood sculptures and trees shaped by the wind. After biking the sinuous road to the entrance of the forested beach path, gingerly walking weathered boards over the boggy ground leading to the cobbled shore, and finally broaching the sweet-scented wild rose bushes edging the beach, I often discover the ephemeral land bridge to Bar Island has vanished underwater.

The tide has turned.

It's not just on the Maine shore that time passes quickly. Time especially speeds up when you have small children. "Don't blink or you might miss him growing up," people would tell me when they saw me chasing after Jake when he was small. But I was too busy addressing the ever-present and pressing demands of a small person—a diaper change, an earache requiring a doctor's visit, a trek to the park so Jake, like a dog, could run off his boundless energy and satisfy his need to explore. I didn't realize that my amazement in seeing my son take his first wobbly steps away from me would evolve so soon into wistfulness when he later walked much further into his own life on other coasts and continents.

I tried to slow down and savor the world as seen through Jake's eyes: his magical thinking that a new pair of sneakers would make him run faster; his imagination turning shadows into roaming monsters and sticks into swords that cut them down; his delight in the ordinary—a bobbing balloon or a chirping cricket would bring him so much pleasure. Especially enjoyable was Jake's insatiable curiosity that led him to turn over dead logs in the forest to see creatures crawling beneath or that prompted him to scamper from one tidal pool to another, looking for suckered starfish.

But more often I was muddled by the mundane—writing articles, making meals, tackling mounds of laundry, walking the aisles of the grocery store, filling out endless school forms, or tending Jake's younger sister. There was not enough time to enter his wondrous world. Except for a few notable milestones, such as riding a bike, driving a car, or graduating high school, Jake grew up without me fully noticing. One minute he was pleading "Carry me" as we walked up the large hill between library and home, and the next minute he was navigating the Tokyo subway system on his own.

The tide had turned.

You don't have to go all the way to Tokyo to go exploring in Maine because when the water ebbs far from the edge of the bay, you can discover the bottom of the ocean and encounter its treasures without even getting your feet wet. While breathing in the scents of wet mud and seaweed, you can search for the rare find: a lobular sea sponge lazing on a gray rock, a piece of blue sea glass glinting in the sun, or the spiny sphere of a sea urchin, the porcupine of the sea.

Even more common sights can startle the eyes—conical limpets patterned in tortoiseshell adorning granite stones and ghostly barnacles crusting rocks with a dull white that contrasts with the indigo iridescence of abandoned mussel shells nearby. Seaweed drapes limply over small boulders like tangled tresses, without a hint of the drama that develops once the water returns. Then these fronds dance upright with the currents, and barnacles extend feather-duster tongues from their beaks to sweep up their microscopic suppers. But at low tide, these sea creatures play dead until the water returns.

Unlike barnacles, most shorebirds find low tide the best time for dining, when the receding water traps fish in the shallows. I try to take advantage of low-tide moments to catch a glimpse of a stately great blue heron seesawing its way along the shore until it quickly gulps up something recently swimming, or to spy eider ducks interrupting their feather-ruffling preening to dive for mussels and plovers pecking at worms just below the water's surface.

Once I saw a bald eagle on the exposed bay plucking meat from a baby seal, its distinctive snow-white head plunging into the scarlet flesh. Likely the seal was too big for the eagle to carry to a nearby tree, where it usually likes to dine in privacy. A friend told me he was driving through the forest in Maine, miles from the coast, when he was startled to see draped across the road a large fish, its silver scales glinting like something out of a Dali painting. He surmised an eagle must have dropped the fish on a flight to its eyrie. But I prefer to view it as a bizarre gift from the heavens.

The quintessential tale about tides is that of the Viking King Canute, who was raised on the shores of the North Sea that surround Denmark. Canute went on to not only rule his native country, but also Norway and England. Legend has it that Canute's courtiers came to admire his power so much that they claimed he also had the power to command the tides of the sea to retreat.

But Canute knew to be humble before the sea that cradled him. To show all that even a king's power is worthless compared to the forces of nature, Canute had his throne carried to the seashore and sat on it as the tide came in, commanding the waves to come no further. Of course the waves splashed closer and closer, sending up sea spray. When water swirled around the legs of his throne, Canute supposedly said, "See there is no king worthy of the name of God, whom heaven, earth, and sea obey." Canute knew that tides are a rhythmic force of nature that cannot bend to the whims of a man, even if that man wears a crown on his head.

A king cannot stop the swelling of a tide, just like a mother cannot stop her son from growing up.

Instead of fighting the tides, you learn to bend to their rhythm when you're in Maine, to follow that pull of the moon. As soon as the tide ebbs, it starts to flow again. Six hours later, the islands return or are completely submerged by water, and there is a new seascape with its own fleeting opportunities for exploration. At high tide you can easily push a kayak into the water and meander the waterways carved in nearby marshes. But you must gauge time carefully; if you return too long past high tide, you won't be able to paddle to shore and instead will have to carry your kayak over slippery rocks.

High tide is the best time to swim in the bay because then water fills it to the brim and there's no need to clamber over the cobbles to reach it. A swim is especially inviting when high tide occurs in the late afternoon. Then rocks and boulders bathing in the sun all day impart some warmth to the water. One friend enjoyed a high-tide swim at 4:00 p.m. the day she arrived at our Maine abode. "This was wonderfully refreshing," she said as she wrung water from her long hair and shook it out of her ears. "Let's swim every afternoon at this time while I'm here." But each day, the times of high and low tide change by almost an hour because of the rotation of the moon around the earth. Her eyes widened when I told her that at 4:00 p.m. the next day we would have to hike out to the water to swim, because high tide wouldn't come until around 5:00.

The constantly changing tides were also an eye-opener to me when I started spending summers in Maine. Back in Philadelphia, I normally divided my day according to the unvarying hours of the clock: I breakfasted and read the newspaper from 7:00 to 9:00 a.m., wrote from 9:00 to 5:00, made and ate dinner from 5:00 to 7:00 p.m., and pursued various relaxing activities until I fell asleep. But once in Maine, it became necessary to observe the tidal clock.

Here you must follow the moon.

To go swimming or kayaking, I have to stop working at high tide. To collect sea glass or explore the islands, I need to close my computer at low tide. Like King Canute, I am ruled by the immense, uncontrollable power of the tides, and I try to match my rhythms of work and play with the ebb and flow of water that follows the moon. This way of marking time makes me more aware of time passing and the need to make the most of every moment.

Yet I also recognize that the tides won't care whether I make it to the islands or to the celery-colored grasses of the marshes. They will come and go, spread out and suck in, keeping the planetary breathing rhythm, the endless time clock, for as the poet Mary Oliver noted, "In water that departs forever and forever returns, we experience eternity."

Nature will go on without me, which somehow is comforting.

The phone rings, and I hear the deep voice of my son, who has gone on without me to live far away on another coast. Many moons have ushered him into adulthood. But Jake hasn't lost his childlike curiosity about the world around him and tries to make the most of his temporary stays wherever his job takes him, exploring each location like a zealous crab scurrying about the Maine shore at low tide. When he moved to California and close to deserts emptied of city lights, Jake bought a telescope and became especially attuned to the moon's rhythms, purposely timing moon- and star-gazing trips to the lunar cycle. Now deep into his twenties, Jake follows not only our moon, but the moons of Jupiter and other nearby planets with his telescope. Although I wish he were here exploring the shore with me, I enjoy seeing other worlds through Jake's eyes.

A friend related to me with some distress that adult children were like wandering pieces of yourself over which you have no control. As I told Jake when he was in high school, worrying about his welfare was part of my job description as a mom and explained why I couldn't sleep well at night until after I heard his key turn in the lock of the front door. But I have learned to let go over the years we've spent apart, to appreciate Jake's adventuresome nature, which led him to visit more than a dozen countries and return with tales of spinning Sufis, Egyptian pyramids, Somali pirates, and almost freezing to death in a hut in the mountains of Croatia. And I've come to accept the temporary nature of the years he spent living with us, recognizing his childhood was borrowed time, for as the Lebanese poet Kahlil Gibran pointed out in *The Prophet*, "Your children are not your children. They are the sons and daughters of Life's longing for itself. They come through you but not from you, and though they are with you, yet they belong not to you." He stressed that the souls of children "dwell in the house of tomorrow, which you cannot visit, not even in your dreams," so parents must view themselves merely as "the bows from which your children as living arrows are sent forth." Like the perpetual tides, my children will live on without me, will sow our lineage far into the future, which somehow is comforting.

A rabbi told me that mothers are closest to their children when they are newborns and recently separated from these beings that once were a part of them. Not used to this separation, mothers still see their babies as extensions of themselves and perhaps this explains in part their intense protectiveness. But there is also something to be gained in the ebbing of the parental pull that occurs as your child grows; the essence of a son or daughter can be seen only at a distance—when viewed too close, it becomes obscured like a pointillist painting.

"The moon was awesome the other night!" my son tells me on the phone, describing all the craters he could see with the aid of the powerful lenses of his telescope. "I know," I said, looking out my windows at a bay emptied of water pulled by the full moon.

I know.

CHAPTER THIRTEEN

Matriarchs and Monarchs

I t is a summer of butterflies.

Colorful fluttering is everywhere. A gathering of blossoms in my garden provides an enticing oasis of nectar in the midst of a forest clearing. Flowers of all shapes and colors line a pink granite path leading from the house down to the rocky Maine shore. The beckoning purple and magenta spires of lupines and butterfly bush that abut the stone steps to the water have the blue bay as their backdrop. Scattered pines, spruces, and firs edge the cobbled beach and tower above the grassy yard, echoing their forms.

But all I can see are butterflies.

The startling indigo eyespot on the taupe wing of a buckeye butterfly stares at me while it drinks. Nearby a series of orange fritillaries speckled with brown line up on a flowering stalk like a regiment, each on its own pink perch of flora. If I get too close, they twirl away, chasing each other up into the sky. Nothing seems to disturb the red admiral butterflies that spiral around lavender veronica spikes, probing each floret with their straw-like tongues. Their open wings are black cloaks edged in vermillion, a few white splotches on their upper flaps. But the most familiar is the most enchanting: the monarch.

Monarchs sail in to sip from yellow coreopsis flowers, their wings like stained glass windows in a cathedral, each orange segment outlined in black. Are they part of the herd of monarchs that migrate all the way from Maine down to Mexico? Or are they allowed only one brief hop in a series of hops that takes their species in the reverse direction, from Mexico to Canada?

It takes three to four generations of monarchs to make this journey of more than two thousand miles. Each butterfly lives about two months and travels only part of the way before laying eggs on butterfly weed and other milkweed species. These eggs enable the next generation of butterflies to carry on the trek north. The final generation that makes the return flight to Mexico can live as long as nine months. As Carl Safina noted in his book *The View from Lazy Point*, "This raises questions much bigger than the butterflies themselves: How do they 'know' what generation they're from and what they are supposed to do?"

Each hopscotching generation of monarchs has the same genetic blueprint, so different genes can't solely explain why the northbound butterflies live only a few months, while the southbound live several seasons. Scientists suspect that certain light lengths and temperatures might alter the activity of specific migratory genes in the monarch to cause the differences in generations. But still a mystery is how the monarch butterfly, over a span of so many generations, knows to return each year to the same forested slope in Mexico to winter—the equivalent of long-dead great-grandparents dictating where their great-grandchildren spend their winters.

My long-dead great-grandparents were Jews in czarist Russia who were restricted to villages known as shtetls. They left Russia to avoid having their twelve-year-old sons conscripted into the army, their daughters raped during the carnage of pogroms. As a child, I overheard disturbing shards of stories about the old country. "Such *tsuris* [woes] we had there, so many pogroms. I was a baby during one and my mother hid me in a dresser drawer," my grandmother told my mother as they ate slices of her still-warm apple cake and I did homework nearby. "Another time my father was coming home from work when someone just started shooting at him. Thanks God he was able to hide behind some trash cans."

Like the monarchs who hopscotch their way across the globe to find better opportunities, at the turn of the twentieth century my great-grandmother and her family packed a few belongings and embarked on a voyage to England and then to America where fifty years later I would meet her—a tiny bent-over old woman in Chicago who always wore a babushka from which only her nose protruded, the rest of her face sunken into wrinkles. We called her "the Old Bubby" and my parents would prod me to come close to her so she could hug me. But I shrank back from this shriveled-up woman who resembled the witches in my picture books.

The monarchs I'm seeing on the move are probably northbound and have laid eggs in my garden. Shortly after they arrive, I spot the telltale bright yellow, black, and white stripes of monarch caterpillars contrasting, like crosswalk markings, with the green leaves of the butterfly weed plants they eat. Monarch caterpillars take only four days to hatch from eggs, and when I first discover them, they are as tiny as a thumbnail, but after a few days of continually devouring leaves, they grow to be as long as a thumb.

Eager to see what happens next, I pluck one of the fatter and longer caterpillars from the butterfly weed and put it in a glass jar, replacing its metal lid with a paper towel perforated by a fork. I add some butterfly weed leaves, which disappear each day into the caterpillar's mouth.

My daughter asks me if we might be harming the caterpillar by holding it captive. Will we disrupt its natural passage into a butterfly? I explain to Eva that as long as we keep the caterpillar supplied with the leaves it has evolved to feed on, we won't stop it from unfolding into a butterfly any more than we could stop a woman in labor from giving birth.

A few nights later the caterpillar stops eating, and before going to sleep, I notice the caterpillar has climbed to the top of the jar, where it hangs motionless from the paper towel lid, the lower end of its body curved so it resembles the letter J. Checking the following morning, I discover no caterpillar but a chrysalis: a surprisingly smooth chartreuse pendant dangling at the top of the jar from what was recently the last pair of its black legs, with a striking bracelet of gold edged with black encircling its conical top.

"Promise me you'll take the candlesticks," my mother said the day she stopped eating. Her pale face framed by short-cropped white hair was gaunt from the cancer consuming her, revealing high cheekbones that had been hidden for years and sinking her large contemplative eyes into a skeletal frame. "I told the Old Bubby I would pass them on to you."

My great-grandmother had brought these silver candlesticks from Russia and I always admired their ornate swirls of etched leaves, emblems of the earth that grounded these objects of piety into nature. Once used to beckon the Sabbath into the Old Bubby's home, the light from these candlesticks eventually had welcomed major Jewish holidays into our own household. I reassured my mother I would take the candlesticks and even promised her I would have Eva polish them like I once did before every Passover. A few days later, my brother closed our mother's eyes for the last time and wept, his shoulders heaving. The workers from the funeral home came and carelessly carted her away, cocooned in a black body bag, leaving behind a profound emptiness.

I brought the candlesticks home that night and wrote my mother's eulogy, marking her passage by noting each important step she took. Attending college in the '40s and marrying my father. Having two children in the '50s. Teaching at Head Start in the '60s, going to grad school during the '70s, and starting a psychotherapy practice during the '80s. It was a full life, but she wasn't ready for it to be over. "Look at all those books I'll never get to read," she said shortly before she died, pointing to a stack next to her bed. "Maybe you'll want to read them after I'm gone."

Once my mother died, the limits of her life—of all our lives—became apparent. Each of us carries out a mere step or two that moves our family forward in time. My great-grandparents took a big leap coming to this country and then worked long hours as a tailor and homemaker so that their son could become a doctor and their daughter, my grandmother, could live a much more secure and comfortable life than the one she left behind in Russia. It's not just candlesticks that get passed from one generation to another. My mother handed off her gift of life with all its unfinished business and imperfections to me, and I will in turn hand off the same gift to Eva; there's just so much each of us can accomplish in one lifetime. But the seemingly impossible becomes possible when all the generations are strung together, each of us playing a humble role in a magnificently evolving lifeline.

The monarch knows this instinctively.

The chrysalis I am harboring continues to hang like a jewel from the top of the jar, small dabs of gold now decorating its tapered bottom. Each day I check it and for two weeks it remains monotonously the same. But one morning I am astonished to discover its light green color has turned an inky black. A few hours later, the chrysalis becomes translucent, and the distinctive orange and black markings of a miniature monarch wing magically surface like a pentimento.

Although looking every few minutes, I somehow miss seeing the butterfly emerge. It has crinkled wings close to its body like the water-wrinkled limbs of a newborn baby. Its chrysalis is now a hollow, clear broken shell. Within minutes, the miniature wings expand, stiffened by fluids pumped into them. At this point, I bring the jar outdoors and remove its lid. The newborn butterfly perches on the jar's edge, waiting for its wings to dry. A few hours later, it flutters and floats up to a nearby maple tree.

The butterfly probably has only a month or two left to taste this world before it leaves the next generation to carry on its migratory pathway. It personifies what Rachel Carson calls in *The Edge of the Sea* "the life force—the intense, blind, unconscious will to survive, to push on, to expand."

Even at the end of her days, my mother was a forceful presence and by no means demure. "Why are you talking to *her* when you should be talking to *me?*" she would say to the doctors in the hospital when they spoke to me about her medical situation.

Hidden under my mother's strident strength was a deep insecurity. Buried inside was a wounded child who held tight to her own child. When I was a baby, my parents migrated from Chicago to the Washington, D.C., area where I was raised. Although she encouraged me to go to the Midwest for college, my mother expected that, like a monarch, I would come back. "Only daughters who don't get along with their mothers move to the West Coast," she said after I told her I was moving to Oregon, a crumpled pile of tissues filled with her tears surrounding her.

No doubt she was remembering when her own mother moved to California, leaving her behind to withstand freezing winters with two small children always sick. My mother always claimed her mother never loved her. Determined to break the chain of that inheritance, she loved me with a fierceness that could be crushing and overly demanding at times. Once I became an adult, I had to tend to that wounded child inside my mother, to make up for the mother who moved away.

Several years after my mother died, I was rummaging through her papers and discovered a version of her will not seen before. *Remember me!* she wrote in her distinctive slanted handwriting at the bottom of an addendum specifying that I inherit my great-grandmother's candlesticks, my brother her wedding silverware.

Did she really think I'd forget her?

I see her every time I look in the mirror—we share an overlapping front tooth and a jawline. She's there when I am reading and writing, her love of literature suffused into my cells. She's there when I am reflective, her need to find meaning embedded in mine. And she's there when I gaze at my own daughter and realize that I must give her the freedom to fly away, no matter how far the distance between us, if it will make her life and the lives of her children better.

My mother especially worried that her only granddaughter would forget her. I too wondered if Eva, only eleven years old when my mother died, would remember a concrete version of her grandmother—one who cuddled and coddled her with a warm embrace—or if the memory would fade into something more ethereal. Shortly after my mother's memorial service, I asked my daughter how she imagined her grandmother. Some people envision loved ones in heaven looking down at the living. Did she see Grandma that way? She was quiet for a moment, put a hand on her chest, and said, "Why would I want to see Grandma as being so far away, when I can hold her close here in my heart?"

The monarch on the maple tree hitches a ride on the air currents headed north. *Bon voyage*, I say, and bring its broken abandoned shell back into the house and place it next to the candlesticks Eva has polished so that their silver leaves gleam in the light. Both the empty chrysalis and the candlesticks remind me of my mother, grandmother, great-grandmother, and the unbroken chain of life that links us all; countless generations of matriarchs and monarchs churned and transformed within the endless spiral of time.

CHAPTER FOURTEEN

Musical Interlude

The transcendental face of art is always a form of prayer.

—John Berger, *The White Bird*

In the glassy bay reflecting a cloudless sky, the music seems ethereal, a rejoicing song that floats up like a prayer to the heavens. These sounds of strummed strings dance through the air expressing a playful joy, in contrast to the scolding of seagulls.

The notes are a little like those of a banjo but pitched higher and less tinny, and certainly not the sounds a guitar or violin would make. *Where are they coming from?* It isn't until I paddle my kayak closer to shore and see my friend Dick's house that I realize he must be setting these notes aloft on their journey out to sea. After retiring from academics, Dick took up the mandolin and plays in a bluegrass band with his piano-playing wife and other local musicians.

Dick has the luxury of time to practice his instrument. But many people are still compelled to tickle the ivories, pluck strings, or blow their horns despite demanding day jobs. Such persistent pursuit of music is surprising and gives a more positive and literal meaning to the term *amateur* (translation: *lover*) rather than its usual, more dismissive connotations. But what do amateur or even professional musicians love—their instruments, the music that comes from them, or something more? What is compelling them to play and us to listen?

When I was a child, I felt music with my entire body, its sound waves pushing me to and fro like kelp swayed by seawater; I would pulsate with each beat. One of my earliest Maine memories is getting dizzy from dancing in circles on the grass, inspired by the cheerful music of the "um-pa-pa" brass band that played every Wednesday night in the old-fashioned, whitewashed wooden gazebo on Bar Harbor's village green. While the adults clapped along to "When the Saints Come Marching In," the children were not content to limit their movements to their hands and instead jumped, cartwheeled, and gyrated to the tuba tooting and the trumpets blaring.

Music has the power to move us so because humans are the only primates whose sound processing system in the brain is so closely married to other parts that govern our movements and emotions. Apes don't dance, so they can't ape their human cousins, who often gyrate to the same rhythm. As the neurologist Dr. Oliver Sacks noted in his book *Musicophilia*, the rhythm of music binds people together because it "turns listeners into participants, makes listening active and motoric, and synchronizes the brains and minds (and, since emotion is always intertwined with music, the 'hearts') of all who participate. It is very difficult to remain detached, to resist being drawn into the rhythm of chanting or dancing." Rhythm, he stressed, binds together the individual nervous systems of a human community.

Once I became a teenager and more self-conscious, I limited my letting loose with music to when I played Chopin nocturnes on the piano. Both body and soul went into pounding out those tempestuous pieces— my torso would rise with each dramatic crescendo, my bottom barely grazing the piano bench, and then I would hunch down when playing the musical resolutions, mimicking how diminuendos shape sound.

It still amazes me that I had the power to unleash the pathos, joy, pride, and other feelings Chopin felt hundreds of years ago by decoding his scratchings—musical notes and notations that captured and preserved the emotions on paper for future generations to unlock. I wasn't experiencing a tragedy such as dying prematurely from consumption like Chopin, but instead was having typical teenage troubles. Breakups with boyfriends. Meltdowns fueled by hormones. Insecurities spurred by unforgiving high school cliques. But to my tender young developing self, who was unable to put anything in perspective and stressed by the slightest provocation, my angst seemed equally consuming, such that it enabled me to musically unleash those same feelings of Chopin's in a cathartic way. The music became a wave that swept away all self-centered concerns into a larger ocean, a shared human tide of feelings that swelled upward, pulling my spirits up with it.

Playing Chopin was a daily ritual and relief, a sort of religious practice during rough times. But it was a practice I soon abandoned after leaving adolescence, only occasionally playing the same nocturnes, but never with as much satisfaction as I felt when younger. Now I play harp, which I started studying in my forties with my then preteen daughter, both of us eager to go beyond piano and pluck the strings of that magnificent instrument.

When we first got our harp, my mother was wasting away from the stomach cancer that ultimately killed her. During the months I took her to chemotherapy and radiation treatments, her full face became gaunt, revealing high cheekbones, and her shrinking body stopped filling her clothes. Her energy also dissipated while the cancer consumed her. Some days she never left her bed. As the author Terry Tempest Williams wrote in *Refuge* about her mother, "A person with cancer dies in increments, and a part of you slowly dies with them."

But there wasn't time to mourn. My mom, whose favorite pastimes were cooking gourmet meals and shopping, no longer had an appetite nor the energy to buy a new wardrobe. So I did the cooking and shopping for her, buying her cashmere sweaters I knew would not get much wear and sweatpants whose drawstrings she could adjust to her shrinking waistline.

While at home, I tried to imagine life without a mother. Without someone calling to make sure I recovered from the flu or to hear the latest exploits of her grandchildren, or dialing my number just to say hello. Except for the beginning of my life and the end of hers, my mom and I spent most of our lives living in different cities, yet we still resonated with one another as we vibrated the telephone lines. My mother provided the regular background beat to my experience of the world since first hearing her heart thumping in the womb. What would our family quartet sound like as a trio, its drummer with the binding rhythm missing? I couldn't handle all the anxiety that thought provoked.

So I practiced the harp.

Not facile enough on the instrument to unleash my emotions while embracing it, I lost myself in another way. Concentrating so intently on finding the right strings and then plucking them properly left little room in my mind for the swirl of feelings sucking me under. Instead of going with the swelling flow of sadness, I rose above it.

There was no rising above it the week my mom was actively dying, which was the same week my brother Joe was definitively diagnosed with ALS after months of uncertainty as to what was causing weakness in his left hand and leg. Ninety percent of all people with this disease are dead within five years of being diagnosed.

Our quartet would soon be a duo.

The night Joe called with this news, my voice quivered as I promised him I that wouldn't let our parents know about his condition and that Dad and I could manage without him until he could join us. Frank was away taking Jake to his college orientation, Eva was away at camp, and my father, always inept around the house, was especially so while his wife was dying. So I took over. For most of that week I tended to my mom day and night. As she slowly slipped away from us, I calmed her whenever she was agitated, made sure she had enough pain medication, and put ice chips in her parched, encrusted mouth when she no longer had the energy to drink. Although functioning well on the outside, inside I was bleeding, the psychological equivalent of a boxer finally receiving too many blows.

That's when I revived my melancholy Chopin.

After Joe arrived and relieved me, I came home, but instead of slipping into bed to catch up on a lack of sleep, I found myself drawn to the piano. This upright had been passed down from my grandmother to my mother to me, its cherry finish nicked over the many years it had served my family. The arthritic piano bench both my mom and I sat on as children groaned in protest as I opened its top and pulled out from inside the tattered music for a Chopin nocturne that was filled with old penciled markings. Although I hadn't played it in years, and the first few bars showed my rustiness, at some point a memory of the notes deeply buried in my mind guided my fingers. They flew from one end of the keyboard to the other, thoughts of the impending loss of my mother and brother compelling them to press the ivory keys more deeply. Swaying to the rhythm of the piece, I was entranced, pouring my sorrow into the piano by releasing undulating torrents of notes, a deluge of feeling, so grateful for a medium to express the ineffable.

The coding for the musical language of feelings appears to be universal, as Diane Ackerman points out in her book *A Natural History of the Senses*. From Australian aborigines to American businessmen, people from all different backgrounds respond to the same passages of music with the same emotions, as evidenced by facial expressions, gestures, and brain scans. For that reason, Beethoven's *Ode to Joy* from his Ninth Symphony can be, as the British musicologist Deryck Cooke described it, an eternal "musical shout for joy" passed down through generations as it taps into something primordial in our minds. Something similar must occur for music performers but in reverse—instead of triggering deep feelings, making music releases them, shaping them into sound waves that carry them away like an outgoing tide. Chopin's nocturnes can be therapeutic for channeling sorrow; his melodies, once evoked by the hands of my mother, now are cathartic for me and my daughter.

What makes this all so ironic are the rational principles musicians must use to stir primeval passions in listeners. The ancient Greek Pythagoras first discovered that the pitch of a musical note is in exact proportion to the length of the string that produces it. What he proposed —and later physicists and neuroscientists confirmed—is that music is precise and mathematical, with distinctive ratios of frequencies needed to create the harmonies we find so pleasing to our ears.

The Greeks suggested these harmonic ratios also were present in the celestial realm, with all the planets in harmony due to musical intervals that described the distances between them. Kepler later modeled his vision of planetary orbits based on this ancient Greek "music of the spheres" concept, claiming that God himself expressed it by harmonizing heavenly motions to create a "symphony of the cosmos."

Eventually astronomers showed that heavenly bodies do not conform to pure musical principles but do follow mathematical laws that predict their orbits. These mathematical laws don't just govern planetary phenomena, but many other facets in the universe from the miniscule to the celestial: from the precise rules governing the spiraling of seashells or ocean waves to the same formulas that determine the spiraling of cloud formations and galaxies. One astrophysicist recently proposed that nature is not just described by mathematics, but is fundamentally mathematical, as evidenced by math equations that prophesized bosons and other subatomic particles decades before they were discovered and by geometry that foresaw the curved shape of outer space centuries prior to Einstein imagining it. Because the universe follows precise rules, physicists can predict the equivalent of the whole pie by looking at just a slice. From the circling of electrons and the spiraling of galaxies, to the rhythms of menses and music, our natural world conforms to a hidden higher order that occasionally gives us glimpses of its brilliant structural beauty.

I find that higher order both inspiring and comforting. It is not merely ballast for loss, but a way to put everything in perspective; instead of focusing on the empty spaces left by my mother and brother—the pauses between the notes—I'm able to see the melody, the sound waves formed by both crests and troughs, the joy that follows sorrow, the sorrow that follows joy, the regular rhythm of waves pounding the shore as the tides ebb and flow, the endless cycles of life that connect me to a vastness of spirit.

The large curved soundboard of my harp is not only beautiful, with its burled maple veneer, but highly resonant. Each time I pluck one of its forty-seven strings, there is a luxurious fullness to the note generated by a number of overlapping sound waves simultaneously flowing in the same harmonic stream. This results in the instrument being musical even when no musical piece is being played. My harp teacher told me that at one of her gigs, after she'd tuned her harp and played successive octaves to ensure they were in sync, someone complimented her on the lovely song.

My harp is positioned in front of one of our sliding glass doors, and on gusty days when the doors are open, a strong breeze from the bay will vibrate all the strings and make faint sounds reminiscent of the harp glissandos often used to signal characters going back in time in old movies. How appropriate, since the breeze also brings in scents of the forest mixed with the sea that take me back to scenes from my childhood: Joe and I scampering on the rocky shore searching for starfish, my mom and I plucking mussels from the rocks on the bay at low tide.

Perhaps when playing the harp, my arpeggios drift all the way out to the water and Dick can hear them as he kayaks by. Sounds travel far on the bay, a small body of water that connects us in more ways than one suspects. I once told my friend Rosemary, who lives with her husband Garry further down the peninsula, that I start mornings in Maine by the water at sunrise, gazing out at the scenery, so thankful for what's before me. She nodded her head up and down as if to underline my comment and said, "You know, my neighbor told me he does the *same thing*."

I imagine both of us by the shore each dawn meditating in unison. We live too far apart (and the bay has too many nooks and crannies) to give a wave or a holler and invite each other over for coffee. But I suspect we are bonded together by a similar morning prayer of sorts that resonates with these thoughts: *Let us be thankful we are here and can experience the beauty before us—that we can spy the heron gingerly wading through the glistening water and the bald eagle flying overhead, that we can hear the squawking of the seagulls and smell the pungent firs, that we can breathe deeply and experience the tidal sighs of the sea. Let us be thankful for another day by the bay.*

But words don't capture the feelings that underlie them, so I take my imaginings further and envision the entire shore dotted with like-minded congregants, who, akin to some ancient tribe, celebrate the sun returning each day—a glorious quotidian feat that is never taken for granted. As the glowing orb rises again, they rejoice by chanting in unison, or perhaps in multiple harmonies, which pile up one upon another, vertically rising to the heavens and transcending all that is earthly; a music of the spheres of sorts that is as moving as an angelic harp song or the notes of a mandolin shouting across a wide blue expanse of water the pure and unutterable joy of being alive.

CHAPTER FIFTEEN

Moment of Zen

Every day / I see or I hear / something / that more or less / kills me with delight / that leaves me / like a needle / in the haystack of light.

—Mary Oliver, "Mindful"

The real voyage of discovery consists not in seeking new lands but seeing with new eyes.

—Marcel Proust, *Remembrance of Things Past*

Nearly every day, my brother Joe tinkered with the world, the world he was leaving.

With a *whirr*, he steered his electronic wheelchair to his computer and used what little ability he had left in his right hand to conjure onto the monitor pieces of the planet—a bee haloed by the sun, luminous scarlet- and orange-tinged Boston ivy creeping across a wall, black tree shadows striping a snowy lawn.

Joe spent hours on each photograph, clicking the proper controls in his photo-editing program so that the view through the camera's lens transformed to the view in his mind's eye. A darkened corner brightened, a harsh color softened, a small part of the image enlarged to fill the monitor, opening up a whole new realm. Some of the photos Joe worked on had been taken years ago before his nerves deserted his legs and forced him into a wheelchair. Other pictures his family took for him. "Don't forget the camera," he reminded his wife, Elke, and me as we left to walk the dog and, by necessity, left him behind.

After slipping the camera around my neck, I took shots of whatever sparked interest along the way—bleached-out beech leaves that were ghostly reminders of the previous growing season, bracket fungi iced with snow, a vase of dying tulips awaiting the compost heap placed next to a pair of more colorful snowshoes.

But it was hard to be a tourist of the inanimate in that Vermont countryside. We were too distracted by following the sound of a nuthatch, the trail of moose tracks in the snow, or by Leah the cream-colored Labradoodle who romped ahead, beckoning us to hurry and see what she saw. We chased after her when she disappeared after a deer, and once we finally caught up, we continually threw her sticks so she stayed close by. Every once in awhile we might stop and snap a picture, but these momentary pauses in our active walk were barely noticeable. We did the exploring, but it was really Joe who did the seeing when we returned, drinking up each image as if it were a spring in the desert.

Joe was always the curious adventurer and some of the photos he played with were windows into that more active world. Choppy water viewed from the rim of his sailboat; ice-capped mountain peaks in New Zealand; the regular rooftops of Paris.

When we were children, Joe and I explored together. While spending summers in Maine, the island's rocky coast was our playground. We scampered over the cobbles in search of starfish or glistening globs of jellyfish and delighted in gathering sand dollars as if they were candies scattered from a burst piñata. Because Joe was the much older brother whose legs were much longer than mine, I was always catching up to him, running over to see what he saw. Once it was a small crab that he put on my head, laughing as I frantically shook it out of my hair. Another time it was a prickly sea urchin placed in my palm.

But when Joe entered his fifth decade, he who was always so adept with his hands found they weren't cooperative when he wanted to turn a key or pick up a utensil. He was losing the nerves that fed his fingers the critical electrical sparks they needed to grasp his fork agilely or manipulate his tools. Soon the nerves that serviced his legs followed suit, making him fall frequently when his muscles wouldn't contract properly.

What most of us take for granted—the ability to move our arms and legs on demand—Joe lost a few years after being diagnosed with amyotrophic lateral sclerosis, or ALS. This disorder destroys all the nerves that mobilize muscles and let you stroll across the room, scratch an itch, turn in bed, embrace a lover, or pet a dog. Most patients die within five years of being diagnosed, often by suicide. ALS is better known as Lou Gehrig's disease because of the famous baseball player who paradoxically told the world he was the luckiest man alive when he was first diagnosed with the condition.

Joe didn't call himself the luckiest man alive. By the end of his life, the only things he could move were a few fingers on one hand and facial and throat muscles, which fortunately let him talk and eat, when fed by others. He, who had always relished his solitude, had to rely on what he called a circus of caregivers to feed, bathe, dress, and toilet him and to frequently reposition him. He also relied on a laundry list of drugs to relieve his discomforts, as well as on his trusty and vital companion—a ventilator he sucked on rhythmically to get the breaths his lungs could no longer squeeze out on their own. With a little bit of ingenuity and the aid of his old Kelty backpack frame, he and his twenty-year-old son figured out a way to strap the ventilator to his wheelchair so the regular *whoosh* of the breathing machine added a bit of harmony to the *whirr* of his wheelchair.

When first discussing the possibility of using a ventilator, Joe put it in the context of his diving experiences. "You need a lot of cumbersome equipment to dive, but it's worth the view you get from deep in the ocean. I feel the same way about a ventilator—it will be cumbersome but worth the view."

And for the most part, Joe did enjoy his view throughout his illness despite his steady decline. Only able to visit him every two or three months, each time I encountered new evidence of loss—a lifeless arm dangling by his side, a skeletal frame devoid of muscle, the sling needed to move him from wheelchair to bed. Another piece of him destroyed by the progress of his disease. Each deterioration was an assault, a series of blows to the solar plexus that took my breath away and made me vacillate between wanting to either cower in the corner or punch back.

But Joe always seemed even-keeled and accepting, at least in the face he chose to show me. Did he mean to guide me through the end of his life like he led me through the beginning of mine? He maintained his measured way of speaking, pausing for each thought to expand, but no longer able to stroke his dark beard going gray. Perhaps dampened by all the drugs he took to relieve his pain and discomfort, there were rarely emotional outbursts. "Aren't you angry and frustrated about what is happening to your body, the unfairness of it all?" I asked him. "Nope," he said, his dark eyes looking directly into mine. "I never believed in a god controlling my fate. I also never thought life was just. I always just had that two-word philosophy: 'shit happens.'"

Joe even had the aplomb to give a lecture to his medical students about his disease and how it was affecting him, how its symptoms revealed the exquisite filigreed forest of motor neurons in the nervous system and which trees had been cut down. The ultimate physiologist, Joe was still in awe of his body even when it failed him and, perpetually curious about everything, even his own impending death.

When Joe was first diagnosed with ALS, I asked Elke how she was able to cope. She quickly responded, "I just don't think about the future." Was it Virginia Woolf who once said she needed to have one of the characters in her book die so others could appreciate life? Some see the glass half empty while others see the glass half full. But Joe showed us something different—how to savor each drop.

The summer shortly before Joe was bound to a wheelchair and then a ventilator, Joe's family and mine shared a cabin on the bay in Maine for a week. Every morning at sunrise, when there was still a chill in the air, we would sit out on the deck overlooking the bay for what Joe called our "moment of zen." While steam rose from our cups of coffee and crows cawed from pine and spruce trees, we would see the morning fog set ablaze by the rising sun and silently share our amazement at the golden world before us. It was one of several moments made more precious by the awareness that it was fleeting.

Like my time with Joe.

Eventually his wheelchair confined Joe to home, but that heightened his curiosity about nature, the view outside. He had his morning coffee in the sunroom, which looked onto a forest of maple trees and other hardwoods. It had a well-trafficked bird feeder attached to one of its many windows. "I keep looking out at the same woods," he once told me, "but it is a nice woods to look at, and each time I seem to find something new. Like that dead birch tree on the edge there. I bet some animal's living inside its trunk and if we keep looking we'll see it."

When we were small, Joe and I used to spend much of our free time playing in the tiny remaining patch of Maryland woods at the end of our block. We lived in a subdivision from the 1960s and, miraculously, that dense vined forest remnant didn't get developed into another split-level home. The wild woods was a magnet that drew all the kids in the neighborhood. We'd gather tulip poplar flowers, work together to build twig forts, and find Indian arrowheads that let our imaginations soar out of the orderly confines of the D.C. suburbs. I suppose the woods outside Joe's windows in Vermont served the same purpose for him. It let him soar beyond a body that wouldn't move, see a world he couldn't fully experience.

But Joe seemed to see things there that the rest of us never noticed. Or maybe we noticed but didn't savor. When first confined to a wheelchair, Joe said he was like someone on the observation deck of a cruise ship—he finally had the time to sit back and relish the view. I rarely had time to pause then, both my writing career and my young daughter requiring most of my time. Rushing to meet work and domestic deadlines, a part of me was jealous of the time he had to observe. Time to see the goldfinches come and go. Time to view fall emerge in stop-action fashion, one leaf set on fire after another. Time to watch the snowflakes drift down from the sky and settle on his lawn, slowly knitting a soft white shroud that muffled sound.

Joe didn't seem to miss the segment of the world he could no longer be a part of—his lab, his students at the university, the mountains he once climbed, the boat he once sailed—nor did he have a bucket list. Instead of anguishing over what he had lost or should have done, the unjustness of a short life sentence, Joe chose to focus on what was immediately around him and to see and reflect upon it more deeply. He had no time for the superficial, no breath for meaningless chatter. "You can come and visit me," he would tell me on the phone, making a point of adding, "but I'm not up to small talk."

The last time I visited Joe was when ALS had robbed him of all movement except talking, swallowing, and taking sips from his ventilator. The nights were the worst. Darkness obliterated the view outside and there was nothing to distract from the discomfort, the pain, the anxiety of feeling trapped inside one's own body. Elke and their two sons took turns staying with Joe during the night, during which they would reposition him every few hours and bend and stretch his limbs. But the lack of sleep was wearying for all of them.

"I don't know," Joe said, gazing out of the side porch windows at the trees around him, his balding black hair just starting to go gray and match the light whiskers in his dark beard. "Once you've been check-mated, what's the point of continuing the game?"

I wanted to plead with him to make his next moves so we could continue sharing our lives. I wanted Joe to be there to reminisce and chuckle over the strange soup our grandmother made when she tried to clean our father's handkerchiefs in boiling water and they disintegrated; to revisit with him the sensation of tadpoles harvested from a Maine pond wiggling in our palms; to remember with him the man in Greece who wouldn't take no for an answer when I spurned his advances until Joe went up to him and said, "Look, this is my sister," recognizing that the only way this man would leave me alone was if another man already had claimed me. I wanted him to help me thrust out the strands of what we shared in our childhoods so that they continued to spin together far into the future. A future in which he could give me his big-brother advice, reassuring me that my mother did the best she could, that my children would get through whatever difficult stages they were in, and that there was more to life than worrying about making a name for one's self.

I wanted all this, but what did *he* want? I kept my selfish thoughts at bay, recognizing how difficult his life had become for both him and his family, how he was imprisoned in a motionless body and unable to make another move. But as once was noted by an ancient writer, *what cannot be said will get wept.*

"Joe!" Elke called from the other room. "Are you making your little sister cry *again?*"

Joe's situation was like the cartoon show we used to watch together as kids. It always concluded with a round black border expanding inward, eclipsing the scene until the screen was completely black and the words, "The End," appeared. Joe's ability to do and experience things was shrinking by the dark rim of immobility, but it left him better able to focus and appreciate the view he still had, like the opening in a pinhole camera. Joe put it another way. "I feel like I'm watching the sunset of my life and the colors have never been so brilliant now that it's about to set," he said, looking up at the colorful mobile of a thousand origami cranes made by his medical students. A symbolic gesture, they were inspired by the ancient Asian belief that folding paper cranes could restore health. In some Eastern societies, these large birds are honored as reincarnated beings pausing on Earth just long enough to help others reach enlightenment.

Years later, I try to pause each morning while sitting by the bay in Maine at sunrise. I gaze out and search for something new in the same scenery, like Monet must have done when he painted so many pictures of the Rouen cathedral. It could be a solitary loon swimming in early morning, leaving a trail of glistening light in its wake. A seal seeking respite during high tide by waddling its way onto our shore. Any interesting tidbit of biology or ephemeral beauty that Joe surely would have noticed, if he were still with me. When finding it, I say, "Here's our moment of zen"—to no one. Then peer through the binoculars to see everything more clearly.

For both of us.

CHAPTER SIXTEEN

Clouds

I once saw cloud streets while cranberry picking on a small island off the coast of Maine. The autumn air was crisp and laden with the scents of sea and seaweed, both sky and water azure and inviting. Scarlet mounds of huckleberry leaves were scattered throughout the verdant blanket of crowberry and cranberry. Emerging from this greenery, like dinosaur bones poking out of the ground, were granite boulders rounded by ancient glaciers. These glaciers also scraped out bowls in the rock in which cranberries like to bathe. After getting my shoes soggy picking a wet patch of these fruits, plump and purple as grapes, I looked up from my crouch and there they were—several lines of clouds fanning out from a distant point like some sort of celestial sign. Could they be the smoky trails jets leave behind? Not that many planes fly by here. Fire smoke? They looked too regular and evenly spaced for that. No, these fluffy stripes were probably cloud streets, avenues to other realms.

Cloud streets are long lines of clouds with blue-sky stretches between them that run in the same direction as the wind high in the sky where they form. Although cloud streets are parallel, they often appear to radiate from a far point on the horizon because of how we perceive them, akin to how parallel railroad tracks appear to merge in the distance.

Perhaps because clouds make visible turbulent winds and other governing forces in the air, they are often symbols of the divine or divine actions. In Exodus, God appeared on Mount Sinai in a cloud and then led the Israelites across the desert in the pillar of a cloud. In Christian scriptures, clouds delivered Jesus and Mary to heaven, and in the Koran, Allah was in a cloud-like state before he manifested. Tibetan Buddhists, in contrast, think you have to rise above the clouds to achieve enlightenment by using meditation. Such meditation, they believe, can take you soaring beyond ordinary concerns, emotions, and thoughts that, like clouds, obscure a clearer understanding of nature.

Although not specifically looking for any divine signs, I spend a great deal of time looking up at clouds when in coastal Maine because its big-sky vistas over bogs, bays, and mountaintops give a daily display of them. Clouds are abundant here because the ample moisture and salt particles in the breeze combine to give birth to them. At dawn and dusk, they soak up the crepuscular crimson, mauve, and orange hues, which highlight their sculptural forms and give the beginnings and endings of our days a depth and golden grandeur. Their diversity and constantly changing forms also make the seascape more interesting than a blank blue sky, as recognized by the Cloud Appreciation Society, whose motto is to fight the banality of "blue-sky thinking."

As the society's founder Gavin Pretor-Pinney points out, clouds often drift by unappreciated by those below. "Most people barely seem to notice the clouds, or see them simply as an excuse to feel 'under the weather.' Nothing could be more depressing, it seems, than to have 'a cloud on the horizon,'" he bemoaned in *The Cloudspotter's Guide*. Deciding clouds deserved more than to be seen as a metaphor for doom, Pretor-Pinney started the Cloud Appreciation Society, whose manifesto specifies that "Clouds are for dreamers and their contemplation benefits the soul. . . . We say to all who'll listen: Look up, marvel at the ephemeral beauty, and live life with your head in the clouds."

This past summer I followed that commandment because, despite the drought we experienced, nearly every day a panoply of clouds appeared on the horizon in all sorts of shapes and sizes: narrow cloud shelves that snuck up close to sunset in an unrelenting linear formation, cloud streets that striped the sky with their fluffy white contours, and even a flying saucer–shaped cloud. One day, while sitting by the water watching the parade of clouds above, I was both dazzled and puzzled. What caused their diversity and rapid transformations, and why weren't they relieving our parched soils with rain?

Clouds have been used as a metaphor to describe the impossibility of knowing God, with one Christian mystic monk proposing that people always will be separated from God by a cloud of unknowing. For centuries, a lack of knowledge about clouds also separated people from an understanding of weather. To note and name is the first step to knowing and understanding something in nature, but how do you name something fleeting? Clouds are the ultimate symbol of the ephemeral, their beauty underlined by their brevity. The unrelenting water cycle that churns salt water in the ocean to fresh water on land thrusts clouds into continual transitions. This dynamic nature made it difficult for scientists to classify these shape-shifters. It was hundreds of years after observers first described the celestial orbits of planets, stars, and other far-flung astronomical feats before a London-based chemist was able to pin down the nature and behavior of those fluffy floating bodies of water much closer to Earth.

Born at the end of the eighteenth century, Luke Howard ran a pharmacy, but he always had a habit of observing clouds, which are nearly omnipresent in the skies above Great Britain. Howard made weather his lifelong muse since he became intrigued as a child by the unusual haze and clouds that formed after two major volcanic eruptions occurred when he was eleven years old.

Howard spent decades sketching the clouds he saw above him, striving to develop a system for naming them that could move the yet-to-be-born science of meteorology forward. Recognizing clouds are water in transition and almost as unstable as steam rising from a teapot, Howard divided them into four basic forms and then combined the names for clouds transitioning from one type into another. It was Howard who devised, in 1802, the holy trinity for clouds that every schoolchild learns: *cumulus*, *stratus*, and *cirrus*, as well as the Latin word for rain, *nimbus*, which meteorologists now use to subcategorize clouds likely to cause precipitation. With Howard's terminology still the basis for our modern nomenclature of clouds, a stratus cloud transitioning to cumulus is called a *stratocumulus*, whereas a cumulus rain cloud is called *cumulonimbus*.

All clouds form when water droplets or ice crystals attach to particles in the air and then are herded together by the physics of atmospheric currents. A cumulus cloud starts as a low-lying cloud but grows upward and outward from a narrow horizontal base, eventually blooming into a floating cauliflower. Fair-weather cumulus clouds are the puffy structures surrounded by blue sky that prompt children or those young at heart to debate whether they are sheep, dogs, ducks, or something more fanciful like dragons. But because convection currents hidden in the air often toss them about like rolling stones, cumulus clouds also come in more tempestuous forms that generate cloudbursts, thunderstorms, and lightning strikes. These clouds are the unpredictable adolescents that cannot control their temper and often unleash furious bouts of rain and hail.

One time while sitting by the bay watching a cumulus cloud parade, I was astonished to see a cloud structure resembling a spinning top or a series of flying saucers that emerged and contrasted with the less defined billowing cumulus cloud below it. By combing through *The Cloud Book* by Richard Hamblyn, I discovered what I saw was a pileus cap cloud that forms when a high layer of moist air is forced up and over a growing cumulus cloud where it freezes into a layer of icy fog. Winds blowing through this pileus cloud can craft it into thin discs that stack up in a regular formation. For similar reasons, similar-looking lenticular clouds cap the tops of mountains.

Stratus clouds are higher up in the atmosphere and tend to be more even tempered as well as more evenly distributed as horizontal cloud shelves (strata) that often completely cover the sky. Unlike the individual cumuli that form when small pockets of warm air rise and cool, bands of stratus clouds form when a large continuous mass of moist warm air rises, often along coasts and mountains, and then condenses en masse into water droplets after hitting colder air above it. Stratus clouds are created by more stable air, so they tend to stick around longer than cumulus clouds and cause less rain. Compared to their cumuli cousins, stratus clouds are much more reserved and regimented, community minded rather than individualistic. Although they can drizzle, they don't sizzle, as stratus clouds lack the dramatic lightning and precipitation of cumulus clouds. But heavy rain and snow can come from clouds hidden above stratus.

One morning I awoke to discover the landscape hadn't—the horizon had disappeared into a blur of gray droplets that hid where sea met sky, so all I saw were the black silhouettes of the fir, spruce, and pine trees and a few feet of the ground in which they were rooted. As

I approached the screen door to see better, I discovered thousands of limpid water drops suspended on the screen, trapped on their entry into the house, and refracting light like diamonds. Others had penetrated, landing on the floor and coating the back of the couch near the door. That's when I realized I was in the middle of a low-lying stratus cloud, otherwise known as fog.

Further up reside wispy cirrus clouds that paint the sky with their soft and delicate brush strokes, creating tendrils whipped about by strong winds as fast as 150 miles per hour. High-flying cirrus clouds don't usually cause any precipitation on their own, but they can signal storms likely to happen soon. "They can be Nature's way of saying that there are changes afoot," Pretor-Pinney notes. That's because cirrus clouds make visible powerful forces in the upper atmosphere that are doing battle in the sky, forces known as warm and cold fronts.

Appearances can deceive, as cirrus clouds, whose Latin name means a curl of hair, are not spun from silky celestial strands, but rather created by the sharp edges of numerous ice crystals that form in the colder upper stretches of the atmosphere. Once when flying, I peered out the circular window of the plane and saw below me a shelf of stratocumulus clouds looking like a herd of sheep crowded together in their pens. Above them, the wind sculpted beautiful drifts of cirrus clouds into waves frozen in mid-curl, like the wave captured by the Japanese artist Hokusai, except that there was a long row of these regularly repeating waves curling in the same direction. These cirrus clouds that formed between winds moving in different directions were the meringue on top of a stratocumulus pie. You can also sometimes see these regularly spaced cloud curlicues looking from the ground upward. Perhaps because they are the highest in the heavens, cirrus clouds have an ethereal quality about them, appearing like "flows of angels' hair," as Joni Mitchell noted in her song "Both Sides Now."

"Wouldn't you just love to pet a cloud?" my cousin Paul said one afternoon when we were admiring clouds floating over the bay. "They look so soft and fluffy." After explaining that those seemingly soft clouds high above us were actually filled with sharp ice crystals, Paul was at first incredulous and then crestfallen. I had destroyed his idealized illusion of a cloud and replaced it with something sharper. He is not the first to scoff at the science of clouds. Thoreau claimed that the scientific explanation for the rosy colors of clouds at sunset—due to the refraction of low-angled sunlight—robbed the imagination while enriching understanding. But with their forms shaped by the currents flowing above us, clouds make it easier to imagine the atmosphere.

Our atmosphere is rare in the universe and should not be taken for granted, many astronauts profoundly realized after seeing our blue planet and its swirl of clouds aglow in the deep blackness of outer space. That NASA image, which upended our view of the world, was also comforting when I was fourteen and struggling with hormone-stirred angst and boyfriend problems. As a way to provide distance, I envisioned flying high above all troubles, away from home, neighborhood, country, until soaring in space and looking down on our planet ringed with clouds. An imagined voice at this point offered a choice: *You can continue to journey in the emptiness where nothing changes, and there are no storms nor sunny days, no emotional highs nor lows, no births nor deaths. In this vacuum of space you can be spared the trauma of loss as well as the joys of embracing life and experiencing it fully, from the deep kiss of a lover to the cries of a newborn, the feel of sunlight warming skin, to the frozen pinch of winter. You can continue to travel in the void or choose to descend back into the body and into a world filled with pain and pleasure, weather both physical and psychological.*

I chose life on Earth.

Somehow consciously making this choice made it easier to bear future hurts and harms because of the understanding that experiencing these aspects of life was better than feeling nothing. Like a favorite sweatshirt, it put everything in perspective; that shirt has an arrow pointing to a star, our sun, in the Milky Way, with the caption "You are here." Yes, we *are* here at this unique moment in time, I remind myself when checking out at the grocery store and looking around at all the people waiting beside me—crying babies, tattooed mothers, men with beards covering their chests, and gray-haired grandmothers missing teeth. This disparate family of humanity is whom I share my world with. One hundred years earlier, none of us was born, and one hundred years later, none of us will still be around. Like an alien who has just landed on our planet, we should be looking around in amazement, rejoicing at what we see before us, in awe of this colorful and vibrant alternative to the void—the dark womb we left behind, the black tomb we'll eventually enter, the vast and sterile emptiness of outer space.

But we don't.

We wait and whine as we absentmindedly read the magazine headlines at the grocery checkout and wish we were *anywhere* but here. Like those bumper stickers that read "I'd rather be sailing."

It may take something life-threatening to make you appreciate being alive. When the final day of my daughter and her boyfriend's visit to Maine arrives and Jason still hasn't had a chance to kayak out to the nearby marshes, I offer to take him. Our bay is calm when heading out, but once we enter the bigger stretch of water where three bays meet, cauliflower clouds appear on the horizon, and the wind picks up, whipping waves in the water.

These cumuli clouds coming off the ocean usually get their start when sunlight beating down creates warmer air, which tends to rise by late morning or early afternoon, sweeping upward water vapor hovering over the bay. That vapor remains invisible until the updraft reaches a higher, colder elevation. There it condenses into tiny water droplets that reflect light in all directions, imparting a distinctive milky color to this weighty cloud that can be as heavy as eighty elephants, Pretor-Pinney notes, yet amazingly is held aloft in the air. Nature can provide us with this magic trick of the fabulous floating cumulus cloud because when water vapor condenses into droplets, it gives off heat that causes the air in the cloud to expand and become more buoyant, like a balloon. The added lift causes the cumulus cloud to grow vertically into the puffy mounds Jason and I see while kayaking out to the marsh.

I am determined to show him the shorebirds in the bay and hoping he will get a glimpse of his first bald eagle. So I ignore the jostling of our kayaks by the small whitecaps coming our way as we paddle a large diagonal across to the marshes, a half-hour kayak ride. Fortunately, the strong sun is warming, so we don't mind the cold sea spray the wind blows back on us each time we lift our paddles. It takes longer than it would have if the water were glassy, but the waves and wind die down once we enter the marsh's inlet.

Following the serpentine route through the marsh grasses, we stop to admire a flock of yellowlegs stabbing the mud on the bank with their long narrow beaks and smaller plovers who fly away in unison, like birds in an Escher painting. But cumulus clouds are starting to pile up and bruise the sky so we turn our kayaks around and head home.

Such rising cumulus clouds often eventually hit a ceiling in the atmosphere caused by a band of air the same temperature as the cumulus cloud, preventing it from rising further. This causes the clouds to spread wide rather than vertically, creating an anvil shape. If enough cumulus clouds form, they may bunch together horizontally across the entire sky, their water molecules bumping into each other and growing into droplets that sprinkle out of the cloud, spitting rain. However, if conditions are right, cumulus clouds can grow amazingly tall, with some as high as Mount Everest. Eventually these tall clouds will reach the upper, colder section of the atmosphere, where they can cause mischief. At that point, the cumulus cloud transitions into a more sinister cumulonimbus cloud. It darkens and its distinctive edges blur, developing wispy protrusions in its upper regions as its water vapor freezes into ice crystals.

Feeling the breeze growing stronger, I'm disturbed to see these signs of an impending storm in the clouds looming on the horizon of the marsh. *This would be no ordinary trip back.*

Now that we're beyond the calming influence of the grasses, winds whip up large waves that we must ride. Up and down we go, small corks bobbing in vast water. It is a vulnerable situation, but there's no time for fear, only time to focus on conquering every wave. I clench my paddle. Despite thrusting as much strength into each stroke as possible, we merely inch our way across the bay. The currents swirl counter to the direction we need to travel. Water splashes into our kayaks.

"Keep going perpendicular to the waves!" I shout at Jason so he won't be tempted to take the quicker diagonal route back home, a pathway more likely to swamp both his boat and lungs with water. Wind whips Jason's long curly locks back into his face and pelts both of us with sea spray. The combination of drenching frigid water and disappearing sun triggers my shivering. The towering clouds threaten to add more moisture to our already sodden clothes.

We are at the mercy of a weather front.

These fronts and the storms they cause arise because of the atmosphere's tendency to use strong winds to even out temperature differences on the planet. Warm air at the equator pushed by these winds repeatedly bumps up against cold air coming from the poles. Because it is less dense, warm air rises over the incoming cold air. When it hits a higher altitude, the water vapor within it cools, forming clouds. If the warm air mass is moving faster than a retreating cold air mass, the boundary where the warm air rises over the cold is gradual, causing a layered sequence of clouds that starts with the telltale cirrus and proceeds to precipitation-causing stratus clouds. But confrontations and displacement of air currents can be more abrupt with steep updrafts, which quickly loft cumulus clouds high into the sky, causing strong winds and heavy downpours.

This is what Jason and I are facing as the neighbors' houses and other familiar landmarks on shore are obscured by distance that doesn't seem to be closing, as if some powerful presence has wiped them off the map, leaving us to flounder in a wake of turmoil.

Various spiritual beliefs often blame clouds or a lack of them on human conduct, droughts seen as stemming from insufficient prayers to the rain gods, and the great flood described in the Bible seen as divine punishment for the iniquity of men. Christian Evangelicals have been quick to blame hurricanes and other natural weather catastrophes on the sinful inhabitants of the areas they strike.

I don't think Jason and I have sinned, yet the ocean continues to pummel our kayaks. Propelled by adrenaline, I plunge my paddle into each wave, while desperately searching the horizon for known forms affixed to the ground—the large white boulder that signals the house down the bay from mine or the pier that precedes it. After a seemingly endless struggle with water, a life-sustaining element whose power I had previously underestimated and certainly never viewed as a dangerous foe, our weathered gray Adirondack chairs finally show up in miniature perched on the edge of our bay. "Follow me!" I yell to Jason, turning the kayak toward the chairs. Nearer to shore, blissfully calmer waters enable us to paddle our kayaks around the rocks and swish into the marsh grasses abutting our stone steps. The flowering lupine and delphinium spires lining the pink granite stone pathway there have never seemed as inviting as that moment when I can finally push out of the kayak and plant both feet on the ground. So elated to be on terra firma again, I almost feel like bending down and kissing the soil the blossoms were rooted into, like my great-grandparents supposedly did after landing on Ellis Island, so grateful to have escaped the roiling waters of the Atlantic and the dangers of pogroms.

In the current digital age, we no longer have to pay attention to the sky like farmers and mariners once did to predict and prepare for weather. Because of how far meteorological science has come since Luke Howard named his clouds, we can now get an online weather report that can predict what weather is coming our way. So perhaps Thoreau was right when he claimed science takes away our imagination and also perhaps our lack of respect for forces of nature.

But it doesn't have to.

If you eye the sky, you can predict a future rain- or snowstorm without the help of a weather forecast. When there is a rise in the air temperature due to a warm front gently sliding over a cold front, wisps of high cirrus are the first clouds to be painted on the blue-sky backdrop or on a canvas with a few low-lying cumulus clouds. These cirrus clouds will build in number and join together, though still allowing the sun to shine through in spots. Eventually, these clouds will descend to create lower-lying stratus clouds that will rain when ice crystals previously harbored in those strands of cirrus become water at the lower altitude. Once they have wept these tears of rain or snow, the stratus clouds might merge with cumulus clouds before breaking up into individual cumulus cloudlets and then vanishing into the blue sky. This progression typically takes a day.

But things become more dramatic when the temperature drops and a cold front, like a rude bully, abruptly and steeply pushes up warmer air in the atmosphere. Once again, cirrus clouds presage the storm to come, only this time they usually clump with cumulus clouds in between wavy striations of blue. This results in a fish scale–like pattern of clouds sailors call a mackerel sky. This cloud formation is due to abundant moisture high in the atmosphere that is being whipped about by strong winds. Soon after, cumulus clouds build in both height and depth and bruise darkly, becoming mountains of water that encounter no ceiling and eventually unleash driving rains, hail, or snow, often accompanied by high winds. These storms, though heavy, are usually brief, the entire storm cycle lasting only a few hours, at which point the clouds break up into patches of stratus clouds and wispy high cirrus clouds.

Either way, it's those delicate, high-up-in-the-heavens cirrus clouds often ignored that signal an approaching storm. Mistakenly thinking the billowing cumulus clouds or low-lying stratus cloud shelves predicted rain, I wasn't looking for the right signals—frail cirrus clouds being blown into curls and fish scales by unseen forces high above. Forces that could turn fair-weather cumulus clouds into storm clouds and bully mild-mannered stratus clouds until they cry.

We now have sophisticated weather satellites and computers that can predict upcoming storms, which as Pretor-Pinney noted, "is a great help in deciding whether to plan a barbecue on the weekend, but it also means that we are forgetting how to read the atmosphere's changing moods. Whilst we are able to watch its expressions, as manifested in the clouds, we are becoming increasingly ignorant as to their meanings. It is as if we are becoming meteorologically autistic."

Was I meteorologically autistic the day I took Jason out on that treacherous kayak ride to the marshes? Did I choose to ignore the ominous signs in the sky and water when we first left our bay because of underestimating the power of weather? These questions came to mind when hearing about another kayaking expedition in our community that did not end so favorably. Ed, who had a family business on our peninsula renting out kayaks and bikes, had taken two New Jersey tourists on a guided kayak ride in the Corea bay one beautiful blue-sky June afternoon. They put in their kayaks at the same beach I had been to at least a hundred times, admiring its beautiful fireweed-framed view of the water speckled by small teardrop-shaped islands of rounded rock topped by evergreens. The same beach I enjoy visiting at high tide when the waves tumble together cobbles on the upper shore so that they clatter like a thousand castanets. And Ed and the New Jersey couple experienced the same sudden and unexpected squall that seemingly crept out of nowhere and caused many of us on land to run for cover.

As experienced a kayaker as Ed was, he and the couple were unable to escape the dangerous combination of wind and water that swept them out into the open ocean. There they were swamped by five-foot waves that capsized their kayaks in 52-degree water. Only one of the three was discovered alive that night by a lobsterman who was part of the search crew sent out when they didn't return on time. Draped over her kayak, her wrist wrapped around a cord attached to it, she was hypothermic, having fallen into unconsciousness while both Ed and her husband died from cold exposure. All three were wearing life jackets.

Usually you chalk up the deaths of boaters, hikers, or other outdoor explorers to inexperience, a lack of the proper equipment, or insufficient caution. But when we first bought our kayaks, Ed was the one who offered lessons on how to recover after capsizing and other sea kayaking tips. He was the one stressing the dangers of the sea and making sure you prepare for them. He was the one who, during his thirty-plus years as a guide, probably had taken close to a thousand people safely through the waters of Corea's bay. If anyone knew what to do during a squall, it would have been him, yet even *he* wasn't able to survive the fury unleashed by a passing storm.

Nature is not always benevolent.

Knowing that already, cognizant of calamities caused by hurricanes, floods, and tornados, I always found it amusing when people were horrified by internet footage revealing fratricides among nesting birds. Such videos punctured their view of nature as warm and fuzzy. But I once saw a snake swallow a frog alive. *Alive.* The snake had snatched the frog by its hind legs and held it tight as the animal lurched frantically to escape death. Then, as the snake's jaws slowly opened wider during a span of about five minutes, they gradually engulfed the frog, its bulging eyes the last to be swallowed. I felt sorry for the frog, but I also empathized with the hungry snake.

After the kayaking tragedy in our own neighborhood, I recalled the explanation given to the ancient Hebrews for why their temple was destroyed and they were unfairly exiled: God had turned away from them. *How could God be so cruel?* Then I remembered my brother's explanation for why ALS was about to cut his life short at the age of fifty-five: *Shit happens.*

Although it follows some predictable rules, weather is not just, cannot be controlled, and can still arise unexpectedly or be ignored at our own peril. I don't believe God is resting on top of the clouds dictating where the rain will fall, the lightning will strike, or the length of a brother's life. If there is a God, then it is one whose motives are obscured by a cloud of unknowing. Akin to Joni Mitchell, I have looked at clouds from both sides now. Seen both their beauty and their brutality, their rules and their irregularities, their yin and their yang, and yet still choose clouds over the empty void.

While writing these words, dramatic weather is unfurling, an autumnal nor'easter roiling the ocean, whipping up a froth of whitecaps on waves that pound the shore and splash against the stone steps edging the bay. Dancing to the beat that raindrops drum onto our roof, towering spruces, pines, and firs in our yard are swaying back and forth while fifty-mile-per-hour gusts splatter torrents of horizontal rain against our glass walls. Wind is whistling through gaps in the sliding doors as well as howling down the chimney, the weather having turned the outdoors into something that sounds like a wounded animal struggling and in pain.

It's weather like this that reminds us of great forces out there bigger than we are, bigger than all of humanity. We are finally getting the drenching rain that has been missing all summer. Rain that will keep forest fires at bay. Rain that will foster a showy bouquet of flowers in the garden next summer. And rain that probably will unleash damaging floods, power outages, or worse somewhere on the peninsula.

There is a two-sidedness to weather you just can't avoid.

CHAPTER SEVENTEEN

Rock of Ages

Transformation is the order of the day for the world: bodies grow and die, species emerge and go extinct, while every feature of our planetary and celestial home undergoes gradual change or episodes of catastrophic revolution. Rocks are a kind of time capsule that carry the signature of great events that shaped them.

—Neil Shubin, *The Universe Within*

I like rocks.

Not the kind of rocks many women like to wear on their fingers, but those that lie scattered on the Maine shore like undiscovered treasures—pink granite rocks with sparkling mineral sequins, smooth black basalt with striking white quartz necklaces, schists with glittering sheets of mica. Drawn to the beauty in stones, I've always been a rock collector. One summer when I was eight, instead of coming to Maine, we went to Colorado where my father attended a research seminar, and Joe and I learned to horseback ride in the forests that gird snow-capped peaks. On weekends we hiked, and I stuffed every unusually shaped or colored rock into my pockets, including those I was certain contained nuggets of gold.

By the end of our stay, I had boxes of rocks—a collection I took pride in and was eager to show off to friends back home in Maryland. But my parents had other ideas, given they had to fit two children, a dog, all our summer clothes, and bags full of snacks into a Rambler station wagon with enough leg room for a three-day drive home. When they told me I couldn't take my rocks, I burst into tears, and after much sobbing my mom came up with a compromise—my dad would chip off a piece of each rock I found, and those chips would form a new rock collection that could return with me. My father spent hours the night before we left cracking apart my beloved stones while I pointed out which piece on each was most important.

I continue to gather rocks from the places I've lived, including pastel-striped sandstone from Wisconsin, amber-smoked agate from Oregon, and mica-encrusted schist from Pennsylvania. But now that I reside on the rocky Maine coast, I want to do more than just collect its stones—I want to understand them. I want to go beyond their beauty, uncover what journeys these rocks took before landing under my feet, learn what forces shaped this unique landscape. Each rock can tell its own tale of how it tumbled onto our locale, akin to travel adventures backpackers from many nations share while holed up at the same hostel.

I want to hear these stories.

I am compelled in part by simple curiosity, as well as by a quest to understand the natural world and my place in it. The deaths of both my mother and brother in so short a span of time were jolting like an earthquake and sent me tumbling. I began to question the meaning of lives so loved but now lost, to doubt the meaning of my own ephemeral life, and to realize that what I counted on so heavily in the past no longer existed. Wanting grounding, something stable to grasp, what better way to find it than to understand the solid ground right underneath my feet.

Often underfoot on the Maine shore are endearing stones shaped and speckled like birds' eggs. Plucking some of these from a beach in Corea near my house, I bring them home to nest on the windowsill. Their smooth round forms suggest a watery past—wave action like a rock tumbler jostled them, wearing down their rough edges. But these rocks were beyond the high-tide mark, so what waves washed over them?

To answer that question, I go on a hike with Acadia Park ranger Kate Petrie. Despite her graying hair, Kate has a childlike enthusiasm for the natural world, and her educational background in glaciers enables her to envision a much different place than what's before us. We meet at Frazer Point, which is part of the small parcel of Acadia lodged on the tip of the Schoodic Peninsula. While walking over large cobbles on the shore, Kate takes me back about twenty-five thousand years, when a massive sheet of ice covered all of Maine. This mile-high ice monster bulldozed its way through the state, scraping off most of its soil and sand and dumping it down south, Kate said. It left behind a rocky shore with distinctive scattered boulders—rocky remnants of icebergs that tumbled off the edge of the glacier and floated out to sea. We can blame the glacier for our frigid waters because it scoured a deep water channel into the Gulf of Maine through which the Labrador Current flows, chilling our bays.

It's hard for me to believe Kate's geologic yarn as she describes seemingly implausible catastrophic events. It's almost like she's a carnival barker except instead of announcing amazing human feats of bendability and distortion, she is revealing the malleability of our world. She tells me the glacier caused major seesawing; its weight depressed the coastal portion of Maine below sea level, and then the ocean extended fingerlike into valleys previously carved by streams and then scoured into U shapes by the glacier. As the ice sheet melted and unburdened the coast of its heft, the seabed rapidly rose and the ocean retreated. But not before ocean waves and glacial ice and meltwater rounded and smoothed numerous stones like the speckled ones high on Corea beach. Kate notes that evidence of Maine's more watery past also can be seen in former sea caves where cobbles smoothed by water can be found more than two hundred feet above sea level in Acadia's mountains—puzzling findings for later-day visitors.

The relatively recent and abrupt downward seesawing of coastal Maine, along with the durability of its granite, explains why its forests are so close to the water's edge, its beaches so cobbled and filled with tidal pools and periwinkles. They are nothing like the sandy beaches to the south, where building sandcastles is a perennial childhood pastime.

Not having sand with which to build sandcastles didn't stop my brother and I from enjoying Maine beaches when we were children. Its tidal pools were like treasure chests for us. We delighted in running from one pocket of water to another in search of the jewels of nature they held inside. "Look, here's one!" Joe squealed when he found a starfish the color of amethyst. Scampering over the rocks to him while dodging glistening globs of jellyfish, I laughed when the starfish he put in my palm tickled me with the prickliness of its suckered underside. The tidal pools brightened the colors of the stones inside them, revealing pink granite with lime green streaks as contrasting as the green grassy strips that divide a highway. The water also highlighted the white concentric quartz rings embedded in basalt the color of the sky deep into the night when no remnants of blue remain. Joe and I stuffed all of these striking stones into our pockets until the weight of them tugged at the waistbands of our jeans. After returning home, we compared and swapped some of our finds as if they were baseball cards, making sure we each had a representative sampling of all the geologic wonders we had gathered.

Years later, it was disturbing how quickly Joe's body petrified, akin to a character from a fairy tale given a transformative curse. Shards of his decline sometimes pierce the surface of my mind: His leaning heavily on my sister-in-law Elke while shuffling from chair to bed, aging the equivalent of decades in just a few months once ALS caused the nerves in his legs to fail. His greeting me at the door in a wheelchair, eager to show off his latest device and all of its mechanical and digital features, as if it were the motorcycle for which he always pined. Although trying to be enthusiastic about it, the lump in my throat was so big I could barely swallow the first time I—the runt in the family who always had to bend back my neck to make eye contact with my big brother—instead had to look down into his dark eyes.

It was wrenching to watch each part of Joe's body seize up over time, but I kept visiting, feeling I had to understand this new person my brother was becoming and what his limitations were in order to best help him and his family. My regular trips to Vermont to see them reminded me of those of my mother, who called herself the flying grandmother, as she determinedly visited each of her grandchildren every few months when they were babies, no matter how far away they resided, because she didn't want to miss their first smiles, steps, and words. But I was watching Joe travel closer to an end point rather than away from a starting point, seeing him take his last steps and hearing his last words. Instead of joyful anticipation before each reunion, there was dread, nearly every muscle in my body clenched on the ride from the airport to Joe's house as I feared what I would encounter, what new parts of my brother had withered away in my absence. It was also bittersweet to see what remained, to see Joe use what limited strength he had left in one arm and hand to massage Elke's tense neck and shoulders, before this limb too petrified.

I know another petrified limb—a black basalt arm trapped in granite at Schoodic Acadia's Little Moose Island, which you can explore only at low tide by walking over a land bridge of barnacle-encrusted and seaweed-strewn cobbles that takes you to a beach bordered by sharply angled blocks of rock. Clambering over these rocks, you can't help but notice occasional long black bands one to two feet wide sandwiched in between coral-colored rock. There you will find the one that eerily looks like a giant's arm embedded in granite, its long black limb ending with smaller, fingerlike projections.

If you scramble further up a path past aromatic bayberry and creeping crowberry and juniper, you quickly reach the open ocean side of the island, where wind whips past your ears and you find even more dramatic scenery—sheer granite cliffs overlooking crashing surf that, along with the glacier, carved out large chunks of their rocky faces. Some of these crags have giant cracks in between them, including what I call a yin-yang pair because on one side of a two-foot-wide gap is a cliff of light-colored granite and on the other side is its black basalt twin.

Moving inland, jagged cliffs give way to a nearly treeless landscape softened by a blanket of greenery. This groundcover is breached by rocky ledge and boulders rounded by the glacier and other water action. During summer, the living emerald and chartreuse blanket is accented by an embroidery of bluebells, iris, and other wildflowers, while in fall, mounds of blueberry and cranberry plants in their autumn finery outline the rocks in striking shades of scarlet, burgundy, and orange. Some of the bedrock ledges have long parallel scratches scored by stones embedded in the glacier that reveal the southeasterly direction the ice monster took as it traversed the island.

No matter how many times I go there, I'm always struck by the strangeness of Little Moose's nearly treeless and boulder-strewn landscape, which is reminiscent of the coastal cliffs in Wales. Years ago Frank and I went on a long misty trek there, while pounding surf below us sent up rhythmic bursts of sea spray. During the entire daylong hike on a worn dirt path through heather, we encountered no one, unless you count those buried beneath us. Every so often we would come across cairns, large versions of the small piles of beach rocks I put on my windowsill. Some were adorned with eroded stone—Celtic crosses marking graves of people who once walked the same path more than a thousand years before.

While walking the path through Little Moose Island, passing the gravestones of former landscapes, I'm puzzled by the island's unique features. What painted those striking black bands of basalt, what cracked the cliffs and created gaps that extend so far back from the island's edge that you have to leap across them at some points along the trail? While tracking answers to those questions, I found myself falling down a rabbit hole of time that led me into strange other worlds. But unlike Alice, who explored a fantasy wonderland full of the topsy-turvy features of an imaginative mind, I was entering real worlds that once all resided right here on our own planet Earth.

My childhood world was dominated by my older brother and parents, who towered above me like mountains. As a small child I lived in their shadows, my gaze always tilted upward, my gait always outpaced. Their legs were so much longer and could travel so much further in one step. I tried to keep up, but they were fast and far ahead of me on the trail when we hiked in Acadia. "I'm *hungry*," I would whine and my mom would stop to give me a snack, but I no sooner finished it when out of my mouth would come a complaint about a cut on my knee or some other calamity to explain why I couldn't possibly walk anymore. A minor scrape took on major proportions aimed at bringing parental attention closer to the ground where I trudged with tired, little legs.

Years later, it was I who would have to slow my stride to match the dragging gait of my parents or brother hobbled by disease, often waiting for them to catch up with their canes, walkers, and wheelchairs, but without the glee I would have felt as a young child victorious in outrunning her family. Compared to that of my brother, my parents' decline was more gradual, subtle, and seemingly endless. During the last year of her life, my mother had several rounds of chemotherapy and radiation therapy that debilitated her along with her cancer until she became bedridden a few months before she died. My father's heart disease steadily slowed him down over several decades, such that by the end of his life, he could walk only a few paces before needing to stop and catch his breath.

But of course I had no cognizance of how time and illness would wear down my parents when I was small, nearing naptime, and we were only a quarter of the way up the trail. "Go ahead without us," my mom told my dad and brother, and she and I walked back down the path at a more leisurely pace, while I picked blueberries and stuffed them into my mouth, relishing each tart handful that essentially was a gift from the last glacier. Before melting away, it left small inland deposits of sand and gravel along with a sprinkling of small boulders that provide the perfect growing conditions for blueberries.

What are the perfect growing conditions for a child? They must vary for each person. But when I was young, my mother seemed to provide the necessary ingredients. Not only did she give us basic physical nurturance, such as home-packed school lunches and home-baked birthday cakes, but she nurtured us psychologically because she saw the world through our eyes. It felt like she was on our team, cheering us on in each of our endeavors, from finger painting to photography, riding a bike to driving a car, and rushing to our aid when either of us suffered or was needy. Once she drove for four hours so I could visit my boyfriend; another time she flew out to be with me when Frank was diagnosed with a life-threatening cancer during college. But after I entered my twenties, my mother's unmet emotional needs and deeply embedded insecurities mounted and began to overshadow our relationship, forcing me to distance myself to prevent being engulfed in her darkness and becoming a target for her anger and bitterness. My mother was similar to the mother Rebecca Solnit describes in her book *The Faraway Nearby*—the one "who gave herself away to everyone or someone and tried to get herself back from a daughter."

When only four or five years old and tired out by hiking, I needed such selfless giving. While waiting for my brother and father to climb the mountain, I sat snugly in my mom's lap, both cushioned and comforted by her full breasts and soft belly, and we sang songs—the wheels on the bus went round and round, the itsy, bitsy spider climbed up the waterspout, and the bear went over the mountain, just like it did in the preschool classes my mom used to teach.

When I was still small enough to meld into the confines of my mother's lap, researchers finally answered the question of why the continents also once fit rather snugly into each other, like related pieces in a jigsaw puzzle, and now were so far apart. Early in the twentieth century, scientists discovered similar fossils, rock veins, and other geologic features in land areas now widely separated by oceans. For example, Maine and other parts of New England have fossils of some of the same prehistoric animals that once roved Europe, South America, and Africa. These investigators then realized that by matching the stratified makeup of the continents' rocky edges—like joining together the lines of writing from a page vertically ripped in two or matching the genetic codes shared by families—they could put the ancient geologic jigsaw puzzle back together, creating atlases of lost worlds.

This research revealed that the continents we've all come to know since grade school as permanent features on our maps were once joined together in a mother continent called Pangaea nearly three hundred million years ago. Then, Maine was closer to the equator and next to what is now West Africa and Europe. Early dinosaurs roamed throughout much of this supercontinent, with no oceans to block their way.

Before these beasts walked their last giant footprints into this earth, Pangaea experienced an extinction of its own continental footprint. Pushed by roiling molten rock under the earth's crust forming the seabed of a nascent ocean, this united family of landmasses was stretched and started to crack around two hundred million years ago. Eventually huge fissures formed and the Atlantic Ocean emerged and continued to grow, splitting the upper section of the supercontinent into North America, Europe, and Africa and their surrounding seabeds, spurring these new continents to drift away from each other. Like the Big Bang, which expanded the universe and sent galaxies scurrying away from each other in the inky vacuum of space, the breakup of Pangaea pushed apart the continents on our ancient Earth, triggering seismic activity in its wake.

So much for being rock solid.

Why did Pangaea and all the other supercontinents that preceded it come into being, only to then disintegrate? The answer to this question lies hidden under the ocean. Although we tend to view Earth as a smooth-surfaced globe, it actually is cracked in several places underneath the sea. These rifts divide Earth into giant tectonic plates on top of which the continents ride and drift when set into motion by slow currents of hot and pliable rock. This motion triggers seabed cracks to regularly burp up magma, giving birth to a spreading new ocean floor that widens the cracks and pushes the plates further away from each other. Eventually the sea crust edges of these drifting tectonic plates will collide, with one sliding under the other and then pulled into the hot malleable underworld of the earth, where it will be heated into a primordial plastic state. Because of this underwater conveyor belt of constantly moving ocean floor, the crust of the earth itself, and not merely some of its rocks, is continually being created and destroyed in an endless cycle.

That cycle thrusts the continents resting on the plates into perpetual motion, causing them to repeatedly bump into each other and then break apart, like a dance that always moves you down the line to another partner. The park ranger Kate stressed that Maine's landscape was shaped by a series of violent collisions and separations—the push and pull of a restless world—and it continues to be sculpted by forces deep inside the earth. "Even today there's stuff going on right under our feet," Kate said, her eyes glinting and a smile spreading across her face, as if she was letting us in on a well-kept secret.

Families too are restless, pushed apart by the expanding geography of competing needs, roiling psychological magma beneath the surface, and ultimately by death. When eleven years of age, I experienced my first family separation as Joe left home to attend a college hundreds of miles away, and we never lived in the same place again. I felt the isolation of an only child—no one to swap record albums with or to share a cynical glance whenever my parents committed the faux pas of their generation. I yearned to have my brother back even if it meant I'd be subject to him taking walnuts from the bowl on the coffee table and throwing them at me as a form of target practice and other minor annoyances older brothers can inflict on their younger sisters.

But I saw Joe only on major holidays during his college years, and mostly on Thanksgiving after that. Once we found our spouses, our households followed different religious traditions so that was the only holiday we shared at my parents' house and then at each other's homes after our mother died. We would gather to have turkey, sweet potatoes, and cranberry sauce while catching up on each other's lives and watching our boys construct spaceships out of Legos. Because Joe's birthday always fell on Thanksgiving weekend, in addition to pumpkin pie, Elke would always make my brother's favorite German apple cake, adorned with candles for him to blow out.

I saw my parents more frequently than Joe after I left for college when I was sixteen, but except for a short period after college, my mother and I never lived in the same city again until the last year of her life. Although we talked often by phone, the different worlds we lived in rarely overlapped, and so, like drifting continents, we gradually floated away from each other, never fully addressing the underlying molten feelings that were pushing us apart.

Though continents drift slowly, it is inevitable that the tectonic plates on which they ride will someday collide with one another. New continental mergers tend to form every two hundred to three hundred million years, often with dramatic long-lasting consequences such as the parallel fractures in Maine's coastal granite formations that give them their distinctive angles and gaps. The fractures weakened the granite so that later-day glaciers easily plucked large blocks of rock off the southern-facing sides of mountains in Acadia as they moved over them, giving these peaks their whale-back shapes.

Massive continental collisions also crumpled ancient rock formed from layers of sediments accumulated underwater over eons. The heat and pressure from these collisions contorted the linear white, gray, and black stripes of this sedimentary rock into a jumble of wavy lines that can be seen in one of the stones on my windowsill. On Little Moose Island, earth-shattering events caused magma to seep up and form long black bands of basalt rock embedded in the granite fractures—stretch marks from gestating new continents.

My mother's stretch marks were jagged white lines that radiated out from the center of her belly, marking my temporary presence within her. She was oblivious to the pain caused by our first separation, my birth, because of drugs given during my delivery. Our second separation, when I went off to college, was more difficult for her, exposing perhaps an underlying depression and an emotionally unsatisfying relationship with my father. But the distance between us eventually closed thirty years later when my mother moved to Philadelphia. During her last summer, I visited her daily, bringing flowers from my garden, stories of her grandchildren, and homemade meals like she used to provide for me. At a certain point in time without me realizing the exact transition, when I was taking her to the doctor, helping her bathe and get dressed, and shouldering the bulk of the responsibility for her care, I became more of a parent to my mother than a child, a mountain more than a cobble. I suppose that is a sign of finally growing up.

My mother welcomed my new role and let go of her bitterness, seeing me perhaps as the loving mother she felt she lacked, the mother she called for when she was delirious toward the end, even though my grandmother had died decades earlier and prior to her death, their relationship had declined to the point that they no longer spoke to one another. The few times my grandmother visited us when I was young, she would always emotionally collide with my mother. The heat and pressure of such confrontations caused fault lines on the past to erupt into angry outbursts and fracturing accusations of insufficiency and unmet needs; the same sorts of arguments my mother tried to repeat with me, but in which I wouldn't engage.

High drama also ensues when continents collide and merge, often triggering mountains to erupt or to be pushed up into existence. About two hundred million years before Pangaea came into being, a chunk of land broke off from another supercontinent and collided into New England. In a geologic instant of tens of millions of years, this collision thrust mountains on Mount Desert Island and the Schoodic Peninsula high into the air. Erosion then gradually wore them down. "It took off their peaked roofs as well as their top two floors, leaving behind just the basement," Kate said.

Over time, the peaks my brother and parents embodied also eventually eroded and no longer evoked awe, all of us operating on the same level once I became an adult, but I still expected my original family to be part of the landscape. Especially Joe, who I assumed would accompany me into old age. You anticipate burying a parent, not a brother.

When he died three years after my mom, my own personal Pangaea disintegrated, setting me adrift like a continent in an unknown sea. I clung to the world left behind and the expectations that my mother would call to hear my latest adventures or complaints and that my brother would hike Sargent Mountain with me again. I heard their echoes on the pine needle–lined forest paths we once shared, sensed their presence in the gaps between granite boulders on shore. Once they died, I realized ghosts were not figments of the imagination, but rather manifestations of a psyche that cannot let go of what used to be. In that sense, ghosts were real and I was haunted by the past.

Six months after Joe left us, his family joined ours to celebrate Thanksgiving. We hustled about, stuffing the turkey, decorating the table with gourds, nuts, and fruit, and Elke carefully placed swirls of apple slices on top of the cake she made in memory of Joe, but it felt like a pretend reenactment of the holiday, a forced celebration. The conversation was stilted and subdued, and at one point, Elke trailed away from the table and I found her later weeping silently on the couch.

We all felt there was someone missing.

Although I was happy to see my grown nephews, when I saw Joe's coal-black eyes staring out of their faces or his square nails on their fingers, I felt a pang of sorrow as wrenching and painful as a rupture of flesh. I didn't want mere pieces of my brother, the chips off the parent rock akin to the stony souvenirs my father created for me from my Colorado rock collection years ago or the Corea cobbles balanced on my windowsill that once were part of mountains. Instead I wanted the whole Joe sitting at our table with his plaid flannel shirtsleeves rolled up to the elbows, while we wished him another happy birthday. The Joe who tormented me with tickling when I was little but later in life offered to drive five hours to Boston to pick up my sixteen-year-old son when he became too ill to continue music camp. The Joe who once raced ahead of me on the path up the mountain when I was a child but then had to slowly traverse Acadia's carriage trails by wheelchair. The Joe who plopped the amethyst starfish into the palm of my hand and then years later used the remaining strength in his own hand to massage Elke's neck. All those missing Joes haunted me like spectral beings whose presence you feel but cannot grasp with your senses.

But over the years I got used to Joe being gone and came to appreciate veins of him running through his grown sons—not just his eyes and nails, but his thoughtful, measured way of speaking, with which his older child makes any argument convincing, and his mechanical mindset that enabled his younger son to fix the espresso machine and realign our cabinet doors. Once the raw edges eroded from the gaping hole he left behind, I mentally collected these remnants of Joe to remind me he is still here with us, though in different form; over time, the feelings they stirred became heartwarming rather than heartbreaking, along with all the memories, all those essential chips that comprise what he means to me. Similarly, though initially I gingerly walked the landscape devoid of my mom, careful to avoid any fragments left behind, I eventually sought them out, mixing old remembrances with the new, the good with the bad, until they formed a fully rounded conglomerate melded with understanding.

Emerging from the rabbit hole, I can now imagine the story of the stones comprising the mini cairn on my windowsill. Some are the remnants of basalt that erupted from the earth's lower crust hundreds of millions of years ago and spent time pushing up between blocks of granite before other forces broke them loose. After being scattered by glaciers and tumbled by ocean waves, they eventually landed above water and in my pocket, along with the granite crumbs of mountains pushed up by ancient continental collisions and the twisted layers of a schist rock whose sedimentary predecessor formed before there was any life on land. These remains of ancient landscapes are reminders of what once was.

It's inspiring how these stones have endured such dramatic changes over mind-bogglingly long periods of time. The twenty years it took my parents to raise Joe and me are nothing compared to how long it takes to raise or erode a mountain. And those rocks I kick around are really the elders of my neighborhood. Our days are numbered and quickly rounded off in geologic time.

We tend to think that what always has been will always be—the earth under our feet, the mountains in the distance, our parents and siblings no more than a phone call away. But permanence is an illusion. The restless nature of our earth leaves no geologic or family formation intact over time—you can't hold on to something moving away. Instead you collect stones left behind—keepsakes of another era, remnants of a brother or mother—and balance them one on top of another, like rocks laid upon a grave, cairns that mark both journey and final resting place, pebbles to remind you of what once was. Nothing stays the same.

But something always remains.

CHAPTER EIGHTEEN

Outfoxed

I have been dreaming about foxes flying.

Ever since reading they can soar through the sky with lunges lofting them airborne as far as the lengths of two parked cars, I've wanted to see foxes flying. The best bet for spying a vulpine lunge is here in Maine, where you often can spot foxes trotting beside the blacktop while looking for their supper. To avoid detection, they track their prey at a distance and then—when some poor mouse is keeping its nose to the ground, minding its own business, totally unaware of the danger that lurks behind it—*Bam!* The fox lunges from its catlike crouch to pounce and pins the animal to the ground.

At least that's what I've read.

I've never actually seen a fox lunge, although a fox is what sealed the deal on our Maine home. We drove up from Philadelphia in the fall to see several properties, one of which we thought might suit our need for a wildlife getaway. This cedar-and-mahogany house was nestled in five acres of forest and had the bay as its backyard. With all of its floor-to-ceiling windows, the house made a perfect viewing post for wildlife, but it needed a lot of work—a new floor to replace musty carpeting, skylights to let in the southern exposure, wood-burning stoves to replace energy-inefficient fireplaces. Would it be worth it?

Frank and I tallied up all the virtues and vices of the house and property while gazing out at the bay from its deck, but we couldn't decide whether to buy it, the lists of pros and cons being equally long. "Let's go on a bike ride," I suggested to relieve the tension of making a decision. We hopped on our bicycles and pedaled the road that wiggled its way past fragrant pines, spruces, and cedars and was occasionally punctuated by the smell of people's wood fires.

"Wow, no cars!" I remarked after biking about six miles without seeing a single automobile. The dense forest was so sparsely populated it must have been good habitat for wild animals, but other than spotting the white rumps of northern flickers as they flew away, we saw no other feathered or furred creatures.

We were almost back at the house when suddenly an ember-red burst of fur flamed out in front of us for an instant and then disappeared into the forest. *A fox!* We took that brief sighting as a good omen—a sign of what we would encounter there in years to come—and promptly made an offer on the house. But although we did see many porcupines, bald eagles, coyotes, and other wildlife the following two summers spent in Maine, when we saw a fox, it was only the blur of its tail as it disappeared into the forest.

Determined to see a fox at closer range three years later while walking on the same road, I am struggling because of my stupidity on a train ride the previous spring. After overhearing an elderly woman fret to her frail husband that they wouldn't be able to heft their bag off the train, I offered my help.

"Oh no, it is *much* too heavy for you," the woman replied, looking down on me, as she was a head taller. But I gallantly insisted I could carry her bag, the song "I Am Woman" playing on the turntable in my head, which was also creating the delusion that I was still as fit as my twenty-year-old self three decades ago when I lifted huge sacks of flour at the food co-op. The woman's bag was almost bigger than I, and after carrying that enormous red suitcase off the train, I was rewarded with relentless intense pain in my lower back that radiated down my leg and still persisted even after several months.

I was no longer twenty.

It is a four-mile walk to the beach, but I think my cranky body can take me there. I walk quietly, hoping a fox won't vanish as rapidly into the forest as it does when I bike or drive by. Perhaps because I am limping, I am especially obsessed with seeing a fox lunge, much like out-of-shape audiences enjoy watching nimble jump shots of professional basketball players. Prior to developing sciatica, I never had any major physical complaints, and minor injuries healed promptly. Being in pain for so long is both frustrating and a little frightening, perhaps portending what might be omnipresent in the near future. Conversations with friends my age or older are increasingly filled with physical complaints—the "organ recital" as we cover the litany of various body parts, from the knee plagued by bursitis to the frozen shoulder.

If I pay attention to my own body, I can sense the pounding pain that surfaces rhythmically like a jackhammer with every step, but the anticipation of seeing the beaver dam at the estuary and then the sandy beach keeps those stabs at bay. Plus, I want to see a fox. *Lunging*.

Most fox lunges are short—up to six feet—but if a fox hunts the downhill side of trails, it can easily hurl itself fifteen to twenty-five feet through the air to capture a chipmunk or vole that never heard the fox until it was pounced upon. By lunging, the fox soars over sticks, leaves, and anything else that would make noise if it stepped on them, enabling a surprise attack.

But how can a fox leap so far? The field biologist J. David Henry answers this question in his book *Red Fox: The Catlike Canine* by noting foxes lunge from a deeply crouched posture, which combined with their long hind legs, helps boost their long leaps. Further enabling their mid-air suspension is their lightness. Compared to most animals their size, foxes have lighter bones and smaller stomachs. Unlike wolves, foxes are nibblers, eating tiny amounts at a time and saving what they can't eat at one sitting for later by burying it in underground caches. A fox is nearly the size of a coyote but weighs half as much.

Foxes are built for soaring.

"It is an action that they have evolved to do," Henry writes, pointing out the fox lunges for the same reason "wolves harmonize in syncopated rhythms and men argue late into the night. . . . Because these actions were meant to be—they are the particular excellence of the species, the pursuit each of us is meant to follow."

Trying to keep the sciatica pain in the background, I walk down the road looking for a telltale flash of auburn. But instead of a fox, there is only the roadside brush strutting vibrant fall colors before donning the more somber grays, browns, and blacks of winter, like performers in the carnivals that occur before Lent. A tapestry of green lichen, bronzed ferns, and pink-tinged moss unfolds over the road embankment and is punctuated by scarlet huckleberry leaves. Any hint of auburn comes not from a lunging fox, but from the leaves of blueberry bushes.

Whether these animals are lunging or not, most people do not look upon foxes fondly in this country, with their well-earned reputation as chicken-coop raiders. Children's stories often depict foxes as deceitful creatures, and the word *vixen* doubles as both a term for a female fox and for a spiteful or quarrelsome woman. But in ancient Japan, foxes and human beings lived close together. This companionship gave rise to favorable legends about the animals, which are seen as spirit messengers possessing the ability to assume human form and become a friend or lover to a person. Like the Japanese, some Native American tribes see the fox as a benevolent figure, as evidenced by folktales in which a fox can become a wise grandmother who nurtures and helps people solve problems.

There's neither fox nor human as I reach the estuary. At this meeting place of fresh and salt water, golden marsh grasses wave alongside a sapphire stream. Sunlight baptizes everything it touches with radiance, sparkling the air bubbles created by beaver and other estuary denizens.

Walking past the meadow studded with the skeletal remains of summer's carefree lupines and steeplebush flowers, I reach the yellowed reeds and beach peas that edge the lip of the sandy beach. There, a splotch of orange beckons, but it is the pumpkin-colored leaves of wild roses. Temporarily giving up my search for a fox, I rest, the sitting relieving the pain, the rhythmic sounds of the surf soothing.

It is low tide and sea debris litters the beach: strands of kelp tossed with rockweeds and the occasional burnished sea glass. A flock of sandpipers skitters across the sand. These shorebirds collectively about-face and scurry, as if attached by invisible strings to the hand of an unseen puppet master who twists and turns them in synchrony.

One of my favorite stories in Henry's book about foxes is that of a kit he observed and named The Prince. When this fox first encountered the ice that had formed overnight on the lake from which he normally sipped, he was initially cautious about the new surface, gingerly walking on top of it. But soon his confidence returned and he resumed his normal trot, which caused him to slip. Puzzled, he trotted again only to slip again. "Then suddenly he burst into a galloping sprint. Legs slipping and sliding everywhere, the fox for a moment was going nowhere. . . . The fox then raced across the surface and came to a sliding, half-stumbling stop, followed by a playful twisting leap into the air. Racing off again in a wheel-spinning start, sliding, sometimes falling onto his side, The Prince had, just like a young child, discovered the magic of ice. From that moment on, ice-sliding sessions punctuated the next several days of this young fox's life."

Henry ends his description of foxes playfully skating on ice by musing, "If foxes and humans can respond to new ice in such a similar fashion, it makes me wonder how many other feelings I might share with a fox."

Soon the Escher-like dance of sandpipers on the beach gets tiring, so I leave and begin the four-mile trek back, more intensely focused on finding a fox along the remaining route. Since there is no new scenery to distract, I feel the familiar ache of a fifty-something back that is reacting to the cumulative toll of walking upright with a skeleton meant to be closer to the ground, like the four-legged creatures from which it evolved. I stop to do some stretching.

And that's when she appears.

She is walking in the distance. Not the usual brilliant auburn, this fox is silvered, her trim black legs in stark contrast to the gray-and-black fur speckled with rust on her body. Whipping my camera out of my back pocket, I shoot picture after picture in case there are only seconds to capture her image before she scampers off, hopefully with a lunge. But the vixen keeps coming closer, slowly trotting alongside the road, her bushy tail drooping behind her. As she nears, I realize her trot is tempered by a limp.

This is probably an old fox that doesn't have it in her to lunge.

I keep taking pictures and soon the fox is right across the road from me. "Are you hurting, old gal?" I call out to her, causing her to stop and turn her head toward me, her bronzed eyes brilliantly gazing out of a face fringed with white fur. Wincing in pain, I squat to take a closeup of the fox, both my knees and back complaining. For a moment, when I am crouched close to the ground and we are locked in a mutual stare and mutual pain, the boundary between her world and mine slips away, and I come to see her as a fellow traveler on the same journey in life who has fewer years in front than behind.

"It's better than the alternative, eh, old one?" I say to her and stand up, flicking my gray hair out of my face. Breaking her gaze, I put my camera back in my pocket. We limp away from each other and continue our autumnal treks, meandering through the moments left before winter snow arrives.

PART FOUR

Out of Eden

CHAPTER NINETEEN

Out of Eden

It would strike around dusk.

Intent on munching the flowers, no amount of chastising would prompt it to leave the garden. After I threw rocks at it, the porcupine would amble away with a swaggering gait, spines menacingly erect. But at night it would return. Unseen but heard—the scritch-scratching of its claws on the tree bark, the rustling in the garden.

After turning the outdoor lights on, I would run out to chase it away, but five minutes later it would return to resume eating my flowers. It was futile—like chasing back a relentless incoming tide. Because of the garden layout, fencing it to keep out porcupines from the nearby coniferous forest and rocky shore wasn't feasible. Spraying the plants with animal repellent didn't work either. And because the porcupine is so omnivorous, narrowing the selection of flowers in the beds was not an option for keeping its damage under control.

I began to regret ever having planted a garden in Maine.

When Frank and I first moved to Maine, I never intended to toil in the soil when I could instead kayak through the marshes where yellowlegs and other shorebirds peck at the mud or hike up a forest-clad mountain where bears and bobcats reside. Why make an orderly human imprint on nature, when it could be enjoyed in its uncultivated and uncivilized state? Better to experience the pure joy, astonishment, and mystery of a wild environment. A garden wasn't necessary in Maine, I reasoned, even though gardening had been a favorite pastime of mine during the decades I lived in Philadelphia.

After we moved north, I kept my hands clean of garden dirt for a few summers. But I missed my Philadelphia flowerbeds and their colorful parade of blooms that started in May and continued through

October. I also yearned to grow species that couldn't survive the relentless heat of Philly summers but that thrived in Maine gardens: flowering spires of lupines, fluorescent-blue delphiniums, and gloriosa daisies, whose burnt sienna centers bleed into a swirl of surrounding golden petals. Perhaps most importantly, I missed the creativity of gardening, the opportunity to paint the landscape with flowers, while also satisfying maternal instincts—the need to nurture living beings and watch them grow to their full potential.

Our third summer in Maine, I could no longer suppress the urge to garden. A friend and her son, both of whom garden professionally, helped me put in three-foot-wide beds on either side of the pink granite pathway that leads from the back of our house to the bay. While swatting mosquitoes, we spent days rototilling heavy clumps of clay, tilling in mounds of compost, and planting close to a hundred small plugs of perennials.

I nursed those plants as if they were my newborns, watering the flowerbed regularly throughout the summer so the tender plugs wouldn't wither in the hot sun. But it was not unconditional love—I was looking forward to the fruits of my labor. While hosing each plant, I envisioned gathering armfuls of indigo delphiniums and golden black-eyed Susans, arranging them in vases with Mexican hat coneflowers, sea thistles, and strap asters. I was like a young mother, imagining myself surrounded by exceptionally handsome and talented grown children, while still cleaning the bottoms of squealing red-faced babies. I weeded and waited for two summers as the three-inch plugs grew into tall, full plants laden with blossoms.

And then a porcupine ate nearly all of them.

I became attached to my garden like my neighbor Larry was attached to his apple trees. A mild-mannered retired linguistics professor who traded his khakis and corduroy jackets for blue jeans and flannel shirts when he moved to Maine from Ohio, Larry has been waging war against porcupines since he planted a half dozen apple saplings in the small cleared patch of forest that comprises his yard.

Porcupines love to nibble on tender new shoots. When his saplings fell victim to these animals, who ravaged the trees with their chomping, Larry was outraged. He'd imagined biting into a crisp, honeyed apple grown on his own soil, but each invasion of porcupines made that vision a bitter unmet dream.

Larry encircled each of his trees with chicken wire. The spiny pests climbed over the metal mesh. Then he built a fence around his entire orchard, but that didn't work either. Even when he electrified the fence, the animals still managed to do damage.

Eventually, Larry took to shooting any of the slow-footed porcupines he saw on his property. "I figure God gave Adam dominion over the animals, so I'm doing the right thing in shooting the porcupines," he told me, his aquamarine eyes glinting under gray brows, shortly after Frank and I had moved to Maine. I was shocked, unable to imagine this retired professor killing such an innocent animal. I had seen him swerving his car to avoid hitting squirrels, and his wife told me he'd once quietly followed the path of a young moose just to get a better glimpse of it. I also was horrified because one of the first thrills of moving to Maine was seeing a wild porcupine amble into our yard. Having only seen them in zoos before, I was delighted to make the acquaintance of this forest denizen, though of course I kept a respectful distance from its cloak of quills.

But porcupines have overpopulated our Schoodic Peninsula. Due to a lack of their natural predator, a weasel-like animal called a fisher, porcupines feel free to roam wherever they choose. Not fearful of their human neighbors, they eat whatever people provide in gardens that border the pine, spruce, and fir forests where the animals live.

They were here first, after all.

Because of their destructive tendencies, Larry offered to shoot any porcupines that came onto our property. "Just call me," he said, "and I'll come over with my gun." Indignantly ignoring his offer, I continued to be charmed by the porcupine climbing my maple tree at sunset. Having been raised on *Bambi*, I viewed shooting animals with abhorrence and certainly didn't feel we had the moral right to kill wild animals unless we needed them for food.

Until I planted a garden.

Each night while I lay in bed, I heard the porcupine: *tromp, tromp, chomp, chomp.* There is nothing quiet or stealthy about its dining.

Its distinctive sound signature is wrought by the animal tromping down the plants and then tearing them apart with its teeth. *Tromp, tromp, chomp, chomp*: the sound grated on my nerves and made it hard to fall asleep. "Dammit! The porcupine is back!" I would yell to Frank, still awake in the adjacent living room. He would then traipse outside and try to shoo the porcupine away with a few well-aimed rocks. But the next morning, there would be a mess of broken or missing flower stems scattered throughout the garden.

I let this floral tragedy continue for several days, mourning each felled blossom. Then I remembered Larry's offer. I was outraged at the destruction, ready to get rid of the spiny pest that was eating my flowers. But what about my ideal of living a wilder life on the coast, enjoying all encounters with the surrounding animals? Maine was supposed to be my Eden, an escape from the monotonous confines of the Philadelphia suburbs, where square lawns and sidewalks suggest order and predictability and no awe-inspiring wild surprises. *The porcupines were here before us*, I chided myself. It is only natural they would be tempted by the buffet of garden treats.

Night after night, I heard the porcupine chewing away at my flowers, and each morning saw new patches destroyed by its voracious appetite. Eventually it gnawed down my naturalist reserve and left a ragged stub of raw blinding anger directed at the animal that was destroying the garden I had worked so hard to build. One morning, after seeing what had been four-feet-tall purple coneflower stems lying prone and wilted on the ground and finding all the flowers missing on my sea thistle plants, I spied the porcupine lounging on a branch of my maple tree, looking quite satisfied with its full belly, its two front paws dangling as it dozed.

Something inside me snapped.

I called Larry. Frank greeted him while I retreated like a guilty puppy to the basement. I had neither the skills nor the stomach to shoot the animal myself.

The conflict was agonizing. I was still enamored with the porcupine and all the wildness it symbolizes—but I wanted it destroyed. Torn between wanting to protect the garden and wanting to protect the porcupine, I didn't emerge from the basement until after the sound of a gunshot. Frank tossed the body far into the woods where I wouldn't stumble across it, but I felt stained by its killing.

Relieved that the battle on my lawn was over, I was amazed at how little remorse I felt. Later I even began to justify my killing by rationalizing that because we humans have reduced the number of fishers—one of the few animals known to hunt porcupines—with our relentless hunting and habitat destruction, we now have a responsibility to keep the porcupine population under control.

Fishers dwell in the northern forests of the United States and Canada. These brown furry animals are the size of a cat but with triangular-shaped, teddy bear–eared faces. To kill its prey, a fisher repeatedly bites a porcupine's spine-free face until it falls over on its back and then will eat the more vulnerable belly. This clever predation strategy used to keep porcupine populations in check, locked in the classic predator-prey ballet in which the porcupine population leaps to higher levels whenever the fisher population plummets. But the mad grab for fisher pelts in the nineteenth and early twentieth centuries, combined with logging of the large undisturbed northern forests where they lived, almost drove fishers into extinction in the upper reaches of the United States. With fishers nearly gone, porcupine populations exploded. In turn, the porcupines caused extensive damage to timber stands.

Seeking to restore ecological balance, in the latter half of the twentieth century wildlife and forest management officials in the United States reintroduced fishers to many of its northern forests, including those in New England. Everywhere fisher populations rebounded, porcupine numbers fell. Although I've heard fishers screaming in my woods at night—terrifying cries that sound like they could come from someone being murdered—these animals still are not abundant enough on the Schoodic Peninsula to keep porcupine numbers down.

Because we've deformed so many predator-prey dances, some biologists argue, we must do our part to ameliorate the ecological damage that ensues. We not only should protect animals in danger of extinction, but also ensure other animal populations (such as white-tailed deer, rabbits, and, of course, porcupines) don't expand exponentially. In fact, some wildlife biologists say the only moral alternative is to restore and protect the natural balance. To do nothing, to let nature take its own course, is irresponsible. Larry's notion of man's dominion over animals may be right—but for reasons other than biblical determinism.

I was first exposed to the restore-and-protect line of thinking in the 1980s when I worked at the International Crane Foundation. In addition to raising these striking stork-like birds in captivity and then releasing them back into the wild, the foundation works with national governments all over the world to ensure there is a wilderness to which the captive-bred cranes can return. A similar Noah's ark approach to saving species from extinction has worked to reintroduce red wolves to North Carolina and golden lion tamarins to certain forests in Brazil.

But what if the problem is a warmer, drier, or more acidic planet due to human activities? The majestic towering California sequoia stands are not likely to tolerate the changing climate conditions experts predict for their extremely limited habitat in the Sierra Nevada. Since these trees can't migrate like animals to more favorable conditions, foresters are now planting millions of sequoia seeds in new locations with varying climates, hopeful they might survive if their ancestors, some of which are as old as three thousand years, succumb to global warming. Researchers are even attempting "assisted evolution" to prevent massive die-offs of coral reefs, which are so sensitive to rising ocean temperatures and acidic waters. Using selective breeding and genetic engineering, scientists are trying to create coral species more tolerant of warmer temperatures and water pollution.

"We are gardening the wilderness," as Jon Mooallem puts it in his book *Wild Ones*. Perhaps we now must be nature's choreographers, acting not just like Adam, but like God.

The day after the shooting, I removed the broken flower stems. Over a few weeks' time, I was encouraged to see new ones taking their place. Other plants the porcupine chewed down to the ground began sending up fresh green shoots. I finally got to see my Mexican hat coneflowers in bloom, their tight swirls of rust-colored petals surrounding elongated thimble-shaped centers, like little sombreros.

But then one night, while I was trying to fall asleep, I heard it: *tromp, tromp, chomp, chomp.* The unmistakable sounds of a porcupine munching nearby. The next day, more broken flower stems were in the garden.

I was clearing out these felled blossoms when I spotted them.

Not one, but *two* porcupines were lying on separate branches in the maple tree. They were smaller than the obese one Larry killed for me— porcupine Bambis—but probably would grow by dining every night at the garden café I provided.

So much for the battle being over.

I still haven't decided whether I'll continue to toil away in my garden, repairing the damage done, or whether I'll ask Larry to kill the new porcupines that have laid claim to my yard. But one thing I know for certain: I'm no longer in Eden.

CHAPTER TWENTY

People of the Peninsula

Originally attempting to "get away from it all" by escaping the human hive of Philadelphia, I expected to have a Thoreauvian romance with Maine—a Walden Pond experience with few human encounters. On our heavily wooded peninsula, you can't see your closest neighbors and have to walk close to ten minutes before reaching their doorstep. That's the way I wanted it, so as to be more fully immersed in nature and free of social expectations and superficial interactions. Wanting to dampen that human tendency to worry about how one appears to others rather than being who one is, I didn't want to feel like I had to wear makeup, uncomfortable but stylish clothes, and shoes that gave me blisters so as to fit in with the flock. I'd rather be silent than have to talk about how unusual the weather is or how those Phillies are doing. As Frank puts it, I tend to be brutally honest, which doesn't sit well with some people. Often not willing to stretch the truth, meld my views to those of others, and continually wanting to delve deeper, I am so down-to-earth I practically sink into the mud. Despite my independent nature, I am still sensitive to shunning by others, which has happened in the past, from the exclusivity of school cliques to the abandonment by those whom I thought were good friends, all of which has made me somewhat mistrustful of the human tribe.

Consequently, I was a little wary at first of the friendly folks who kept dropping by unannounced to introduce themselves the first summer we spent at our Maine home. But then I ran out of printer paper, a vital necessity for a writer. "No problem," my neighbor Carol said as she gave me a ream to tide me over until my next trip in town. And after a birch tree blew down in a storm, blocking our driveway, I was thankful when our neighbor Larry traipsed over in the pouring rain with his chainsaw so he and Frank could move it out of the way. It also was a pleasant surprise to see my stooped-over neighbors, Stan and Roberta, then in their late eighties, plod down our gravel driveway, arm in arm. They had come to deliver some wild cranberries they had picked on their property that I later folded into a cranberry-orange bread to share with them.

I began to welcome these interruptions of our solitude, especially when stormy stretches kept me indoors for days. If rain incessantly drummed on the roof, I was eager to catch up with my neighbors and relieved when the telephone rang with an invitation to meet over a steaming bowl of soup or cup of tea. Running out the door, there was no need to put on makeup or change out of a stained sweatshirt or jeans with holes in the knees. Nobody cares.

The unexpected virtues of our community were further underlined the summer I wanted to fill my newly created garden with flowering plants. Although I already planted many small plugs of perennials purchased from a nursery, there were still several large gaps that needed closing with flora. I tell Carol about my search for flowering plants. "You don't need a nursery," she says with a laugh. "Just go over to the Jacksons'. They've got a bunch of perennials in their garden they're always dividing up that they can give you."

Carol introduced me to Mel and GayLynn Jackson at a Fourth of July party at her house, but I didn't know them well. They moved to Maine from Connecticut when Mel retired from his job as an engineer. Mel was known as the "beaver man" because he was in charge of maintaining the private dirt road that leads to our housing development. That meant he collected money from all of us to pay for graveling. It also meant he often could be seen at the road's culvert pulling out brush the beavers use to dam the estuary that flows through it.

A few years ago, the beaver dam sparked controversy in our little hamlet by the sea. Blocking the flow of water, the dam frequently caused floods on the road, forcing costly repairs. Some people in the neighborhood think it a worthwhile trade-off for seeing the rustic stick lodge of the beaver and all the waterfowl and other wildlife drawn to its pond. But others are unhappy about the frequent flooding of the road that necessitates taking a longer detour off the main thoroughfare.

To pacify these individuals, Mel and other neighbors disassemble the dam to restore normal flow to the stream. This task is never-ending because the beaver then repairs its lodge with frenzy, often rebuilding in a day what is taken down. (The sound of trickling water acts as an instinctual trigger for dam-building behavior by these animals, which depend on the stagnant water their dams create for protection from predators. Researchers found that beavers will cover a tape recorder playing the sound of running water with sticks and mud, even when the tape recorder is on dry land.)

Others in the beaver brigade gave up, but I often saw Mel's tall, lean frame pulling branches from the culvert. Determined to fill my new garden beds, the next time I biked by him, I asked if I could see his garden. "Sure," he said, a shy grin spreading across his face. A few days later, he and GayLynn, like proud parents, gave me a tour of their flowering perennials, which blanket their entire backyard, a hill that slopes downward to the bay. It reminded me of Monet's impressionistic paintings of his flowering estate in Giverny. Bright magenta dabs of rose campion flowers dotted a backdrop of gold-and-rust black-eyed Susans. Indigo and pale yellow spears of foxglove pierced the sky nearby, while patches of astilbe plumes waved soft smidgens of pastels and creams in the foreground. But unlike Monet's garden, which was accented by a bridge over a pond, Mel and GayLynn's garden was accented by the glittering blue border of the bay. "I wanted to make sure I'd never have to mow a lawn again," Mel said with a smile, providing a modest explanation for a gorgeous garden.

Before leaving, I let Mel and GayLynn know that if they ever thinned out any of their flowering plants, I'd love to put them in my garden. To my surprise and delight, a few weeks later I came home to find more than a dozen of the plants I'd admired sitting in pots in my driveway, and a message on my answering machine from Mel advising me to plant them soon.

The next floral gift came courtesy of Ozzie. Always sporting a baseball cap, a ruddy complexion, and cheerful energy, Ozzie is known on the peninsula for the delicious apples, peaches, and plums he grows and sells. As a second career he picked up late in life after working as a school teacher and then fisherman, Ozzie lovingly tends dozens of dwarf fruit trees on the grassy slope next to his house, which has a distant view of the ocean.

When Ozzie saw me carrying a few perennials purchased from a vendor at our local farmer's market, he offered to help. I told him I bought the perennials to put in my new flower garden. "Aw, you didn't have to do *that*," he said, shaking his head, almost indignant. "I've got *lots* of perennials in my garden needing thinning that I can give you." The next time I picked up some of Ozzie's plums at his orchard, I took him up on his offer of plants. Expecting a few, I was amazed to see him dig up a sampling of every flower he grows, including phlox, gayfeather, anemone, and coreopsis. It was worth five times what I spent on his plums!

The generosity of our neighbors also can be seen in the winter when we're not there. One January, after offering to go inside our house to make sure there weren't any problems, our neighbors Larry and his wife Mary discovered a leak in our chimney. After Mary cleaned up the water on the floor, Larry, who was well into his eighties then, and another younger neighbor climbed onto our roof and tarped the chimney for us.

The surprising munificence of our neighbors probably stems in part from the isolation we experience here, nearly an hour's drive from stores offering a decent selection of plants, groceries, tools, or other needed supplies. This isolation has fostered its opposite—a merging of human resources and the mentality *if you don't have it and I do, I'll give it to you to save you a trip and someday you'll return the favor.*

The year-round community in Maine is especially attuned to the mutual dependence they have on their neighbors. Some of these seemingly provincial born-and-raised-in-Maine folks actually are cosmopolitan in their widespread welcoming of all sorts of humankind, no matter their creeds or sexual orientations. Way before there was general acceptance of homosexuals, gay couples migrated to Maine, where they were warmly received, for the most part, with Maine one of the first states to legalize gay marriage. And though Maine is one of the whitest states, an original founder of the Schoodic community was an African American freeman who moved here in the late eighteenth century.

The respect natives here have for others with different viewpoints seems to rub off on the summer people and year-round retirees that populate our peninsula. In Philadelphia, I tend to congregate with like-minded people, with many of my friends Jews like myself with leftist politics. But up in Maine, my closest neighbors, Larry and Mary, are Evangelicals who lean far to the political right.

Always attired in blue jeans, Larry spends much of his time tending his forest and garden and going clamming. Larry's wife Mary is an artist who does oil paintings of the area, including three that are hanging on my walls. I often go over to see her latest endeavors while sharing a fragrant cup of licorice-flavored coffee. We catch up on what our daughters are doing, what books we've read, what warblers we've seen, and where to find wild chanterelle mushrooms or cranberries.

I can count on Mary to give me some flour or milk until I get around to going to the store, just like Frank can count on Larry to help him take trash to the nearby dump in his rusty old red pickup truck. Even though our political and religious views don't overlap, we do share a love of the beauty and nature around us. As my neighbor Roger pointed out the first time we had a meal with Mary and Larry, "There are certain things we just don't talk about around here."

Remembering that comment one night, I enjoyed a delicious Middle Eastern feast on the Jewish New Year that was prepared by one of my neighbors—Mazouz, a Muslim Palestinian who moved to Maine from Massachusetts when he retired. We brought Ozzie's apples to ceremonially dip in honey, and Mazouz made a separate batch of his meatballs without yogurt sauce, in case we were kosher. As I ate his delectable baklava and heard him reminisce about the Palestinian village he grew up in, I was tempted to ask him what happened to that village when the Israelis took over the country, but I held my tongue.

Many of the natives on the peninsula also forgive people's shortcomings to an astonishing degree. One summer while doing work on our house, our contractor Alan experienced a tragic death in his family. His father was lobster fishing, he told us, when another lobster boat rammed into his, throwing him overboard and into a watery grave. The captain of the offending lobster boat was a young man who had apparently set his boat on autopilot while he ate his lunch and wasn't as attentive as he should have been. "I knew the fellow and knew he had been having problems with his drinking and his marriage. I'm a good Christian, so I reached out to him," Alan told us, stroking his red beard that made his penetrating blue eyes more striking. Shortly after the memorial service, Alan offered his father's accidental killer his forgiveness and tried to foster the man's forgiveness of his own self.

Perhaps it's good religious values at work, but I suspect the locals recognize they will be keeping company with each other over several generations, sharing the same plot of land before and after their deaths, so they try to make the most of it. One woman on the peninsula told me she was the twelfth generation of the Tracy clan to live in the area. Many people here can make similar claims, with the Tracys, Youngs, and Crawleys putting their names on everything from lobster stands, gas stations, and markets, to roads, wharfs, islands, and gravestones. Joe Young told me his ancestors sailed to Corea on a sloop to avoid the draft during the war—the 1812 war. The only white people then in Corea, he claimed, these original Youngs welcomed the first Crawley who washed ashore after his British ship wrecked on the shoals. That Crawley married the Young's daughter, establishing the first of many connections between the locals that live in this still sparsely populated area. Those connections span multiple generations as well as saturate the current cohort. Young told me that during prohibition, his grandfather was arrested for bootlegging. But this Young convinced the sheriff minding him in the jail to set him free for the night so he could attend a local dance. The dealmaker was the promise that Young's wife would bake the sheriff one of her renowned berry pies.

It would be confining for me to grow up and stay in a place where people still call you by the nicknames you incurred in grade school, with an underlining expectation that you haven't changed much despite decades passing since you graduated. But I can see how being accountable to a stable community can instill better behavior. Contractors and other workers will not do shoddy jobs because they know word travels fast in a peninsula where everyone knows you and will find out if you don't do good work. And you try to get along well with your neighbors because chances are you may need their help the next time you lose power or your car breaks down.

Such accountability can be quite effective in small societies, noted Yuval Noah Harari in his book *Sapiens*. Studies show that in groups that number fewer than several hundred people, "There is no need for formal ranks, titles and law books to keep order. Below this threshold, communities, businesses, social networks and military units can maintain themselves based mainly on intimate acquaintance and rumormongering," Harari writes. Perhaps that's why few people bother to lock their doors here.

Of course the Schoodic community, like any human enclave, has its share of conflicts and petty resentments. There was the bitter rivalry that erupted before my time between inhabitants of the two main roads in my housing development over which dirt road would get paved first. And there was the woman who complained to the town office that her neighbor's rosebushes were too high and obstructing her view. Another resident successfully lobbied the township to fire our policeman because he was annoyed by all the speeding tickets given by this man with whom he went to high school. And recently there was the loose cannon who took it into his own hands to solve the flooding road problem by shooting the beaver. There's probably lots of dirt under the surface I have yet to uncover. Despite their economic dependence on the tourist trade, there also must be some born-and-raised-here folks who resent the increasing influx of retirees and summer folk like me who dominate their surf and turf. "Nobody's from he-yah any mah," bemoaned the crusty guy at the lobster coop when he overheard me talking to one of my neighbors about driving up from Philadelphia.

But some of the small kindnesses these locals extend to even short-term residents and visitors are phenomenal, from the just-picked and sweet-as-candy cherry tomatoes the house painter brought us, to the eagerness to be helpful that our postmistress showed Frank when he made it to our local post office right after she closed it. "Oh, I can open it up again for you," she told him cheerfully as she let him in to get our mail. "This would never happen in Philadelphia!" he responded. Just to reach a person by phone at the Philadelphia post office often requires a hold time of more than a half-hour, and by the time you reach them, neither you nor the person on the other end of the line is cheerful. Similarly, when I check out at the closest major grocery store, the bagger assiduously separates all the food that has to be refrigerated and puts it in my cooler and bags the rest. This is all done with a smile, something that would never happen in our city of brotherly love.

The generosity of the people of our peninsula became especially apparent after a fire one spring burned down the barn of a saltwater farm many of us depend on for our produce and other groceries. Bill and Cynthia Thayer started Darthia Farm in the 1970s. They were back-to-the-landers who left both possessions and professions—insurance agent and teacher—in New York City to make a living raising and selling organic produce, poultry, pork, lamb, eggs, and homespun wool. But in one night, the fire killed all their horses, sheep, and pigs, and nearly all their cows and chicks. The Thayers didn't have enough insurance to cover the damage done, but the community ensured their farm would continue, preventing a tragic situation from becoming a tragedy. Friends, neighbors, and local organizations held several fundraisers, as well as donated money and their own animals and lumber to the Thayers. Businesses in the area also contributed. Then there was an old-fashioned barn raising, with dozens of folks giving their time, tools, and carpentry skills to rebuild the barn in a few weeks' time. Tears came to my eyes when I came to Darthia Farm to buy my groceries and saw in front of its beautiful new barn a sign stating in big letters: *Darthia Farm—Rebuilt by Human Kindness.*

Is it just the sparseness of the population here in Maine that fosters such kindness? Studies show that the more overpopulated experimental rat populations become, the nastier they are to one another, with overcrowding leading to greater fighting and neglect of progeny. Does that mean the less populated a community is, the more it is likely to induce kinder behavior? Of course humans are not rodents and similar research done on human crowding has generated conflicting findings. But surely how crowded we feel in an environment also must affect how we interact with people.

Or could it be how much strangers comprise whom we encounter that determines how we behave? In our community in Maine, walkers not only say hello to everyone they meet on the street, but wave to every passing car on the road. All those drivers wave back or stop their cars to say hello, because whomever you see is either someone you know or someone you ought to meet. In contrast, the only people besides my immediate neighbors who have said hello to me when walking the streets of Philadelphia were those few strangers I came across during a major snowstorm. This reminds me of a quote from an Icelander in a guidebook I once read who claimed, "A small community expects a lot from each individual, and each individual's contributions are also more likely to be noticed and appreciated."

You do feel more noticed and appreciated in Maine, despite being hidden in the environment and despite encountering more people during one walk in Philadelphia than you'll encounter in a year spent living on the Schoodic Peninsula. Dwelling in this rural community has made me see the better side of human nature, including my own, which, like the bent-over birch trees you see up here, has become more pliable, with branches that reach out and touch others. I also realize that all my lofty ideals fostered by the nature memoirs I've read can carry me only so far when there are more pressing needs close to the ground that only the people near me can meet. This is something even Thoreau knew. Contrary to the myth perpetuated about his Walden Pond experience, while living there, Thoreau was within walking distance of Concord. Rumor has it that he made frequent trips back to this home base—so his mother could do his laundry.

CHAPTER TWENTY-ONE

Out of Place

W e've been invaded.

First it was the mice that broke into our Maine house over the winter and presented us with a houseful of droppings when we returned in the spring. Then it was the large black ants that paraded down our rafters carrying hundreds of white eggs that they scattered all over the floor, along with the sawdust they created. The next day, we discovered a large pool of urine some unknown animal left next to our welcome mat on the deck, presumably an attempt to mark its territory. But the latest invasion is even more unsettling. Pulling out of the driveway, I hear the unmistakable sounds of a scurrying animal inside my car.

I panic.

Here I am, a nature lover who seeks out all sorts of encounters with wildlife in the Great Outdoors. I will crouch in one position for long periods of time, while mosquitos feast on all exposed body parts, just to get a flash of fluorescent orange from a warbler flitting about a pine tree. One early morning when fog blurred the far edges of a bog and dangled water drops like jewels on a filigree of brush, I stayed motionless despite my aching back so I wouldn't blow my chances at seeing a moose. Stumbling upon a garter snake in the garden, I relished the sighting and continued to pull weeds alongside it despite a genetic inheritance that should make me afraid of such sinuous encounters.

But the thought of meeting up with an unexpected visitor inside my Toyota makes me squeamish. Bursting out of the car, I yell for Frank to do some wildlife exploring within it. He soon discovers the rustling is coming from a red squirrel scampering among empty grocery bags in the back seat. Opening both back doors, he shoos it out, but while driving I worry another animal might appear suddenly in a pop-goes-the-weasel way.

The next day while walking downstairs to do the laundry, I think I see a red squirrel in the window well but then realize with a jolt that it is on the *inside* sill of the window. It scurries out when it sees me, and I just as quickly run in the opposite direction. Once my heart stops beating so fast, I walk upstairs and find some duct tape to repair the dryer vent hose the squirrel had ripped to make its entry.

That same day, while I am out and Frank is working in the office, he hears scratching sounds and discovers the squirrel has ripped through the living room screen door. After chasing it out, he tapes up the hole left in the screen. Thank God for duct tape.

Why do I enjoy seeing wild animals so much outside the house but get so perturbed seeing them indoors? I could blame everything on the damage they do inside—the fecal presents, torn screens, chewed woodwork. But there is probably something more at play—finding a wild animal within your house or car disturbs your equilibrium, your sense of place, the sharp division between their world and yours. We seem to have a self-centered instinct that it's okay to enter their territory, but it is much more intrusive for them to enter ours. But what is the appropriate territory for a wild animal? And what is the appropriate territory for me?

Context is everything, I realize one day, when a chance convergence totally upturns my view of natural pests. It is high tide and a gaggle of Canada geese appears out of nowhere and silently swims before me on the calm bay like a perfect graphic design—a straight line of repeating black-and-white forms. It is a sublime moment of zen, yet back in the suburbs of Philadelphia I am continually cursing these overabundant birds. They traffic to the few man-made ponds in the area, leaving me to dodge their omnipresent droppings that speckle the grass, and if I come close to one of their nests, they honk and run toward me in a nasty attack mode. Is it just the largesse of the bay or the aptness of them swimming in this natural body of water that stifles my resentment and restores the wonder?

Although I enjoy spotting wildlife in my Philadelphia suburbs, it is disconcerting when a deer walks down the sidewalk there or a wild turkey scrounges around my bird feeder only a few feet away from the front door. Greeted with both these scenes recently, I found it degrading for the animals, akin to seeing one of your neighbors transformed into a homeless person desperately seeking spare change. The Philadelphia area is not the only metropolis that wild animals are invading. Feral hogs root through city parks and private lawns in Houston and Atlanta, black bears splash in backyard pools in suburban Los Angeles, polar bears cross city streets in northern Russia, and coyotes hunt for prey in New York City. A fisher was even spotted in the Bronx, and one raccoon scaled twenty-three stories of a skyscraper in St. Paul in a bizarre twist of its natural instinct to climb trees to escape danger. Particularly pathetic was the coyote that got trapped inside an elevator in the Federal Building in Seattle. It was chased in there by crows trying to protect their fledglings.

You can't blame the animals—there's no place for them to go.

Urban, suburban, and farming developments over the last century or two have substantially shrunk the habitats of deer, foxes, bears, coyotes, and wild turkeys. Similarly, green way stations filled with the native berries and fruits that birds like to dine on have become few and far between, and most meadows once dotted with wildflowers that sustained butterflies are now orderly rows of tulips, hedges, corn, or soybeans. In the 1950s, 30 percent of the world was forested. Now less than 5 percent is.

As someone who grew up in a new housing development in the Washington, D.C., suburbs back in the 1960s, I have seen close at hand how intrusive we can be. Nearby forests and fields rapidly transformed into neocolonial homes and lawns when I was a child. Real estate developers filled in creeks I used to enjoy wading in, panhandling for the sparkling pieces of mica I thought were gold. They paved over the tall meadow grasses that shielded us when we pretended we were Apaches hiding from the cowboys. They cut down the prized climbing trees that let small children reach enormous heights. The bloodroot and Virginia bluebells that reappeared with the first warm breeze of spring no longer popped out of the leaf litter. Eventually the once extensive natural areas where all of us neighborhood kids would gather together to build twig forts, find arrowheads, and carry out our make-believe play vanished. These havens for wonder were replaced by sterile, unimaginative new houses, all of the same mold like in a Monopoly game, and bland blocks of grass. It wasn't just suburban sprawl, but a bona fide catastrophe for both the wildlife and the yet-to-be-tamed children who lived nearby.

So convinced that all this precious wild land was disappearing, I put away the first few coins I earned babysitting to save some natural plot of earth from similar destruction. So in a way, I achieved a long-term goal when we finally bought our slice of Maine forest and shoreline. Now I can see a statuesque great blue heron forage for fish in the bay, which is a much more uplifting scene than a clumsy turkey at a bird feeder. Deer hide in the forest rather than trot down the sidewalk. But that doesn't stop a painful awareness that protecting five acres does not go far enough in ensuring the large swathes of green space many animals need to prosper and not be nuisances to their human neighbors —places where the wild things are.

As a species, we are inordinately pushy and domineering, literally bulldozing down anything that gets in our way. Probably no single organism has changed the planet as much as we have. Scientists estimate that people have transformed more than four-fifths of the land on Earth that is ice-free, earning our current geologic era the moniker Anthropocene. Those transformations have been accompanied by mass extinctions of animals, and not just in recent times. When early humans first left Africa, they left a trail of destruction everywhere they went, prompting the extinction of giant kangaroos, marsupial lions, dragon-like lizards, and many other large animals in Australia, as well as the extermination of giant sloths, saber-toothed tigers, mammoths, and camels, to name just a few of the many species who met their demise once humans entered the Americas. "The first wave of Sapiens colonization was one of the biggest and swiftest ecological disasters to befall the animal kingdom," notes historian Yuval Noah Harari in *Sapiens*. The advent of agriculture caused even more annihilation. "Long before the Industrial Revolution, *Homo sapiens* held the record among all organisms for driving the most plant and animal species to their extinctions. We have the dubious distinction of being the deadliest species in the annals of biology," Harari stressed.

Is it hopeless to think we can do a better job playing with others on the natural playground, or are we instead destined to be the eternal selfish bullies who lack empathy, a sense of fairness, and feel entitled based on a notion of superiority? Maybe it's not haughtiness but separateness that keeps us from sharing, an inability to see that we are cut from the same cloth; that inviolate division between our world and theirs that made me gasp when I saw the red squirrel cross it.

The falsity of that division becomes apparent after I hear the primatologist Frans de Waal speak about his research on bonobos, which he calls the hippies of the primates because of their free love tendencies; these apes use sex to solve any conflict, even those arising between animals of the same sex.

But de Waal didn't come to talk about monkey sex. Instead he talks about the universal abilities of primates to reconcile, be empathetic, have a sense of fairness, and all the other traits needed to be moral and take an ethical stand. In one video he shows, a researcher gives a monkey a tasty treat after performing a certain task, while the monkey in the neighboring cage is given a second-rate food after doing the same job. When this monkey sees his neighbor chomping on the more desirable grapes, he has what in a human might be called a hissy fit. He screeches and shakes the bars in his cage to express his frustration at the unfair world the experimenter offers him. I, along with most of the people in the audience, laugh at the uncanny likeness of this monkey's temper tantrum to that of a child denied a treat his brother got or some other similar human scenario.

It's not just primates who have a sense of fairness and are empathetic, de Waal shows us. In the next video of research done by Inbal Ben-Ami Bartal and Peggy Mason at the University of Chicago, by nudging a gate open with its snout, a rat rescues a fellow rat trapped in a plastic enclosure. Even when tempted with a similar enclosure near the trapped rat that is filled with a tasty chocolate treat, rats are just as likely to first free the trapped rats and then share the chocolate with them as they are to first lift the gate of the container with the chocolate and indulge in the food. Although the liberating rats could choose to eat all the chocolate first before freeing the fellow rats, they were more likely to share it with the freed rats, revealing a surprising degree of generosity.

As if that isn't startling enough, de Waal, who calls himself an "apathist" because he is apathetic about religion and doesn't care if there is a God, takes these findings further to conclude that man created God in his image and not the other way around. Who needs God to tell us how to behave if our sense of ethics is inborn or culturally learned? If rats can do it without God, so can we.

"If that's the case, what makes us unique—what traits do we have that lower animals don't?" asks a young bearded man at the lecture with pleasant expectation on his face.

"Not much," de Waal responds with a frown, noting that a lot of our behavior has elements of those animals below us on the evolutionary tree and that there wasn't an aha moment when we came on the planet, but rather a gradual honing of what came before us. Some animals share with us the ability to plan ahead, make and use tools, count, and have abstract symbolism, otherwise known as language, although they may not be as picky about syntax as we are. Even animals low on the evolutionary totem pole have cognitive abilities akin to ours. Fish use tools, hunt cooperatively, respond to their reflections in a mirror, and remember things they've seen a month previously, studies show. Paper wasps have brains the size of pinheads, yet even they have the ability to recognize each other's faces.

De Waal coined the term *anthropodenialism* to describe our common rejection of humanlike traits in other animals or animallike traits in us. He claims that when our ancestors became farmers, they lost respect for animals and began to look at themselves as rulers of nature. To justify how they treated other species, they had to play down their intelligence and deny them a soul, he stresses. As he wrote in a *New York Times* article: "The more we play down animal intelligence, the more we ask science to believe in miracles when it comes to the human mind. . . . In our haste to argue that animals are not people, we have forgotten that people are animals too."

So there was no aha moment when humans evolved. Instead, the aha moment is that we aren't the pinnacle of creation and the world doesn't spin around our little finger because we are so special. Galileo showed us this, Darwin showed us this, and now de Waal tells us again, in so many words:

We are not the center of the universe.

I become an intruder in another universe the same day I encountered the red squirrel in my car.

It is exceptionally hot, so I drive to a friend's swimming hole, a small abandoned quarry surrounded by maple, birch, and pine trees. Approaching the water and peering in, I spot a flurry of small minnows followed by a large scarlet-flecked fish. As it swims by, its gauzy fins edged with luminescent cyan undulate among the tadpoles. But that doesn't deter me from jumping in and experiencing the sudden rush of cold water that instantly relieves the heat. Refreshed, I float on my back and admire the sheered faces of rust-and-black-stained granite topped by towering fluffy white pines that cling to the crag. Light reflected on the rippled water dances on rocks above, while damselflies stitch their way through the air with their striking blue-and-black-striped needles.

After swimming for a while, I make my way to the edge of the quarry. When about to climb out, I suddenly come eye-to-eye and less than a foot away from a frog as big as my fist. As surprised as I am, it freezes, giving me time to admire its lemon throat edged in emerald green and the sparkling copper rim around its large black pupils.

What does it think of me? Is it as perturbed at finding me in its pond as I am at finding the squirrel in my house? Does it find me out of place? I hope, if it has some sort of sentience, that it thinks there's room enough in the quarry for both of us, just as I have to acquiesce there's room enough on my plot of land for both the red squirrels and me.

Perhaps I should take lessons from Ozzie, my friend with the fruit orchard. Ozzie thought someone had been robbing him of his apples because one morning he discovered a tree had been picked clean of fruit, with none of the broken branches that porcupines, raccoons, and other animals leave when they ravage his trees. Determined to catch the thief in action, Ozzie put up an outdoor camera that is triggered to take pictures when it detects motion. A few nights later yet another tree had been robbed of fruit, so Ozzie looked at his camera's pictures, eager to see who the thief was. But although the camera had caught the culprit in action, delicately picking each apple from the tree, Ozzie saw not a human, but a bear standing on its hind legs.

"So what do you do when you discover a bear is eating your apples?" I ask Ozzie while picking fruit from his trees.

"You share," he responds matter-of-factly, putting several russet apples into my bag.

I try.
    I read up on red squirrels to find something endearing about them. (Did you know they clip and gather mushrooms and other fungi and place them in tree branches to dry in the sun? I once saw a red squirrel with a yellow mushroom cap four times the size of its head clutched in its mouth.) But neighbors continue to tell me about the damage these animals do—how they ransack pantries, chew through the electrical wiring of houses, and make themselves at home in people's living rooms, sitting on the sofas as if they were designed for their comfort alone. In short, they do a form of human habitat destruction that can't be reconciled and triggers instinctual human hissy fits over unfairness akin to that of the monkeys in the video de Waal showed us.

So although recognizing the seeming generosity of the frog, the altruism of the rat, and the desperation of the suburban turkey, I remain unwilling to share my domicile with red squirrels. But I'll try to respect their right to romp in the yard, making their signature alarm-clock calls, and leaving their pilings of pine-cone brackets. They are as much a part of the Maine landscape as the blue herons in the bay.

Despite my frustrations at the squirrels and other animals that ventured into my house this year, I need to remember they were all here prior to we humans. Before they trigger territorial instincts, raise my blood pressure, and bring out an inner playground bully, I need to slow down, take a deep breath, and realize one important and indisputable fact:

We are the invaders.

CHAPTER TWENTY-TWO

Shoreline Cleanup

"Head for the island straight ahead," yells Becky, pointing to one of several outcroppings in the distance that resemble porcupines with fir and spruce trees on their backs instead of quills. Eric, Joe, and I paddle our kayaks as directed, following Becky's lead in the water. Seagulls screech at us as they fly overhead, and the wind whips the ice-cold sea spray coming off our paddles back into our faces. It's a brisk fall day, the sky weighed down by leaded clouds, and we are embarking on another shoreline cleanup in Maine, wary not of the waves, wind, and a potential rainstorm, but of what we will encounter across the bay.

This is the kind of beachcombing where you hunt for trash rather than treasure and unbecoming sea debris rather than luminescent sea glass. We are like archaeologists plying the middens but disturbed by what we're finding. One third-grade teacher who participated in the last cleanup cried when she saw all the trash that had collected on the islands. After she came back, she arranged for a volunteer with a boat to take her schoolkids out to see for themselves what happens when you treat the ocean like a garbage can. Eric tells us he was kayaking the other day behind a lobster boat and saw a steady stream of debris being thrown off the stern, from bleach bottles to candy wrappers and soda cans.

Some of the trash from lobster fishing is unintentional—storms sweep up lobster traps and buoys along with the ropes between them. This wasn't such a problem years ago when the traps and buoys were wooden and the ropes hemp, both of which blended into the landscape and rapidly decomposed when they beached and then bleached on shore. But now the ropes and buoys are made of more durable plastic that doesn't biodegrade nor seem to lose its garish primary colors.

Colorful plastic also coats the metal traps all lobstermen use these days, as well as comprises the bait bags inside them and the rubber bands they use on the lobsters' claws. Consequently, unnaturally colored mounds of rope and scatterings of bait bags, buoys, rubber bands, and storm-bashed traps persistently wreathe many of the islands' shores, marring the beaches of Maine's many peninsulas, their plastic leaching out toxic chemicals, their unnatural shades jolting the eye.

Some of the plastic trash has nothing to do with lobster fishing. During the last cleanup, Becky pulled from forest brush a deflated silver balloon with "Happy Birthday!" inscribed on it in bright blue and yellow bubble letters. "They should outlaw these Mylar balloons 'cause they *never* decompose," Becky muttered as she shoved it into her trash bag. "People should use the ones made out of cornstarch."

If not purposively dumped at sea, a practice still prevalent among some countries, plastic trash is often blown out of open landfills, tossed onto landscapes and seascapes by litterbugs, or enters the ocean after being washed down sink drains in the form of the microbeads used as scrubbing agents in many soaps and dental products. Shipping accidents also enable plastic to enter the sea. A major storm besieged a ship when it was in the Pacific Ocean midway between Hong Kong and Seattle, causing the notorious loss of an entire shipping container, which spilled out more than twenty-eight thousand plastic tub toys. Once sprung loose, these modern-day equivalents of rubber duckies then embarked on epic journeys, floating their way to shores as far north as Siberia and Alaska, where beachcombers found them. Due to similar accidents, small pellets of plastic used in plastics manufacturing often land in the ocean, which sprinkles them on shore where they become permanent plastic debris that environmentalists call mermaid's tears. More prevalent are plastic bags, which, next to cigarette butts, are often the most common item of trash found on beaches. Plastic floats far and wide in the ocean, so even remote beaches are not free from it. We think of the Arctic as being pristine, but researchers found an island in the Arctic that had an average of one plastic item every three feet of shoreline and that concentrations of plastic mermaid's tears were greater in the Arctic Ocean than in any other ocean in the world. Some researchers estimate that there are more particles of plastic in the ocean than stars in our Milky Way galaxy.

Becky organizes shoreline cleanups on the Schoodic Peninsula several times every summer and fall, motivated to keep the beautiful shores there from becoming contaminated by toxic trash and the broken dolls, umbrellas, and other unbecoming human detritus she's seen ruin the white sand beaches in the Caribbean, where she vacations in winter. With a long tawny braid tinged with gray and a face etched by years spent mostly outdoors, Becky is a back-to-the-lander who built her own log cabin in Maine forty years ago with her husband Art. Enamored by Maine's forests and seascapes, she tries to capture them with her watercolors and has resisted having indoor plumbing in her house because she says she would miss seeing the moon shining through the firs at night on her way to the outhouse. A gardener and forager of both Maine forest and sea, Becky depends on a healthy and awe-inspiring natural world for nourishment, both physical and spiritual, hence her commitment to shoreline cleanups. I too am motivated to clean up our shores, not just to rid them of the buildup of lobster traps and trash that are environmental contaminants and eyesores, but because I am haunted by something much smaller, more widespread, and much more insidious—*plastic sand.*

When scientists first figured out how to spin their strands of plastic from liquid concoctions in the early twentieth century, these chemical wizards had no idea how quickly they would transform our world. The more durable and less expensive plastic was soon used to replace natural biodegradable materials, from the silk in stockings and the wood in toys to the metal in cars. But what made plastic favorable for manufacturers—its long lifespan—has made it problematic for the planet. It takes 450 years for plastic bottles and disposable diapers to break down and even longer for plastic bags, which some estimate require a millennium to fully decompose. "Plastic bags are a product with a useful life measured in hours and a waste life measured in centuries," notes Edward Humes in his book *Garbology.* Americans now throw out more than sixty times as much plastic as they did fifty years ago.

But plastic thrown out does not necessarily mean plastic that disappears.

As Ian Frazier noted in a *New Yorker* article, "Science learned long ago how to put together hydrocarbon polymers to create plastic, but it still has not found a good way to take them apart. . . . Unlike wood or paper or the human body, a plastic bag does not decay to the basic elements it used to be before it took solid form. Even broken down to microscopic crumbs, plastic will still be plastic."

Exposed to salt water, sun, and surf, the plastic debris floating in the sea shreds into tiny pieces that act as chemical magnets for toxic substances such as PCBs and other pollutants and become what Humes calls "floating pockets of concentrated nasties." These plastic particles also leach out bisphenol and other compounds that can wreak havoc with the reproductive systems of animals and cause cancer.

Plastic particles ultimately become broken down into colorful plastic confetti that makes its way to the shore where it piles up, creating toxic, durable plastic sand for the sandcastles of future generations. Some beaches are so contaminated with plastic that their sand resembles the colorful gravel seen at the bottoms of decorative fish tanks, Donovan Hohn noted in his book *Moby Duck*, which documented Hohn's pursuit of the floating bath toys spilled into the ocean. "What's most nefarious about plastic is the way it invites fantasy . . . the way it is intended to be thrown away but chemically engineered to last. By offering the false promise of disposability, of consumption without cost, it has helped create a culture of wasteful make-believe, an economy of forgetting," Hohn writes. Only 5 percent of plastic products are recycled and the equivalent of five plastic grocery bags filled with plastic enters the ocean each year for every foot of coastline in the world, a number made scarier by the fact that it is on the rise and that ultimately this plague of plastic will result in plastic sand. *Plastic sand!* I shudder to think what beaches will be like for my grandchildren.

I don't have any grandchildren yet but think of the next generation when on my hands and knees in the forest picking up pieces of Styrofoam. When we first landed on the island, it looked relatively free of debris, but then Becky noticed a line of baby blue Styrofoam crumbs creating an aberrant pathway from the cobbles on shore into the spruces, as if pieces of sky had fallen and become embedded in the ground.

Because it absorbs the odors of fish, the unnatural appearance of Styrofoam doesn't stop birds from thinking it is food, and their pecking at it creates the plastic crumbs we see scattered in the forest. Many marine birds and fish die from ingesting plastic particles, including the poster child for plastic pollution, an albatross chick from which was recovered more than 250 plastic items, including cigarette lighters and bottle caps. These items were featured in a poster Greenpeace made with the startling title "How to Starve to Death on a Full Stomach." Another sobering photo captured by an underwater photographer was that of a seahorse clutching a pink plastic Q-tip in the curl of its tail.

"Shit!" Becky says, her hands on her hips and a scowl on her face. "We can't possibly pick all that Styrofoam up." But I suggest we give it a try, and both of us crawl on the ground, spending about ten minutes using our fingers to rake it into piles we could then scoop into a black trash bag.

While we're raking we hear Joe shout out, "Oh man, look at this!" With a full head of hair starting to go gray and round wire-rimmed glasses, Joe is another back-to-the-lander who homesteaded in Maine the same time as Becky and once worked as a guide for kayak tours into wild areas. We follow his voice to discover him standing next to a large piece of blue Styrofoam that probably ripped off a dock and is still intact—sort of. When he picks it up to show us, blue Styrofoam dust sprinkles down to the ground. "Look at that," Joe says disgusted. "That's going to make it back into the water and become lobster food." He also shows us an old television and the rusted front grate of a car. He leaves both where he found them because we can't possibly carry them back in our kayaks.

What we can tote back easily are gallon-sized bleach bottles, and after returning to the rocky edge of the shore, we find there's one of these big bleach bottles about every twenty feet. Lobstermen use bleach to clean their buoys on board their boats, and many then throw their empty bottles into the sea, as if that makes them disappear. We untangle some of the rope we find washed ashore and use it to create long strings of bleach bottles that will float behind our kayaks on our return to the mainland. "I just wish the lobstermen could see this," Becky says, taking a picture of the bleach bottle tails we are dragging behind us. Becky once went into the local elementary school to talk to the children about pollution in the ocean and asked them, "Why do you think lobstermen throw bleach bottles out of their boats?" One boy shot up his hand, so pleased that he knew the answer. "Because they're *empty!*" he told Becky triumphantly.

Environmentalists debate the value of shoreline cleanups. Some promote them because they not only clean the beaches but make those picking up trash more mindful and less likely to use and carelessly dispose of a water bottle or some other common trash item. Other environmentalists think it wiser to forge policies that prevent the trash in the first place rather than those that involve picking it up. Such policies include making people pay for the plastic bags used for their purchases at stores or banning them outright. The average American throws away five hundred plastic bags a year, most of which cannot be recycled because they jam recycling equipment. Fighting that rising tide of plastic pollution, many cities as well as entire countries charge fees for the bags or have banned their use, both of which have noticeably decreased plastic bag use and litter. Just a five-cent fee on plastic bags in Washington, D.C., led to about a 60 percent decrease of bags found in its Anacostia and Potomac Rivers, and after China banned thin plastic bags, bag use in the country fell by forty billion bags a year. Even more comprehensive is the European Union's ban of ten single-use plastic products that most often end up in the ocean. These products include straws, cutlery, plates, and cotton swab sticks, in addition to bags.

Beyond advocating for plastic bag bans and other laws aimed at stemming the rising tide of plastic products, we can all do our part to prevent the buildup of plastic sand by reusing, recycling, and refusing plastic disposables that truly aren't so easily dispensed. Vendors can pour coffee into the reusable mugs we provide rather than into Styrofoam cups and pack our groceries into reusable cloth bags or bags made of cornstarch, which decompose. We can drink tap water and carry reusable water bottles instead of buying the sixty million plastic water bottles that Americans throw out each day. Every plastic bottle we reuse is one less bottle likely to beach onshore.

And we can do shoreline cleanups.

After strolling the cobbled beach picking up bleach bottles, we find a stretch of brush that Becky calls the mother lode because it has trapped an abundance of soda bottles and cans, motor oil containers, the bright blue plastic gloves lobstermen wear, rope, buoys, bait bags, lobster traps, plastic bags, and other miscellaneous trash. After two hours, we have filled close to a dozen large black trash bags and made several strings of bleach bottles. Joe looks over our collection. "This is good—look what just a few people were able to gather in just a few hours," he says. "But it's also bad," he adds, shaking his head.

This time there are no lobstermen to help pick up the trash bags and traps we collect on shore and haul them away on their boats. The first time we did a shoreline cleanup, Becky contacted many of the lobstermen in the area to see if they would be willing to haul away the trash on their boats. Despite most of that trash originating from their fishing endeavors, only one lobsterman agreed to help out, perhaps due to the time-consuming and exhausting job lobster fishing entails during peak season. Many lobstermen also seem to be either in denial as to the problem of trash on shorelines or resistant to helping out for fear that shoreline cleanups will foster greater awareness of the problem, leading to government regulations that would cramp their independence. Even Becky's husband Art, a first-generation lobsterman, didn't volunteer his boat to help haul trash, not wanting to raise hackles in a fishing community where multiple generations of fishermen can be cited like a biblical lineage.

You do have to respect that tradition and the hard work of the men and women able to make a decent living trapping lobsters. Lobster fishing can be lucrative, and although it is rife with danger due to boat-sinking squalls and mishaps with ropes, it can enable a person working independently or with just a few helpers to support a family comfortably. But can any of us truly be independent of the ocean that sustains us? Aren't there limits to what our blue planet can endure before we all suffer as a consequence?

On that first cleanup, we couldn't possibly kayak back with all of the large busted lobster traps weighed down with bricks that we found on the island, so Becky had us build a tower of them, which would make an obvious environmental impact statement, a monument to any boaters passing by, lobstermen included. After that, more lobstermen were willing to help with our cleanups.

But there are no lobstermen helping today and the sky is gunmetal gray as we strap trash bags and tie bleach bottle tails to our kayaks and then finally push off from shore. The wind has picked up, making small waves that occasionally splash into the opening of my boat, drenching my bottom half with frigid water. Our small kayaks are barely noticeable once we enter the open ocean, tiny bobbing lines of red, yellow, and green on the slate-colored expanse of water, just as our cleanup efforts will no longer be noticeable when we return next year to find the shore ringed with a new batch of detritus.

PART FIVE

Meaning behind the Matter

CHAPTER TWENTY-THREE

Fall Migration

It's early September, so I have yet to shut out cold nights with closed windows or take the chill off mornings with a fire in the wood-burning stove. But the wildlife is already sending signals that summer is coming to a close and that fall, with its great southern migration, is on its way. Even the vegetation is in flux. When hiking through the heath yesterday, I noticed the sphagnum moss was beginning to blush pink and the green of the grasses has worn away to reveal a warm undercoat of yellow. Eventually these colorful carpets will gain the mottled orange and scarlet hues of the berry bushes, a fall tapestry that reflects the colors of the frequent fires we make in autumn.

There's a contagious restlessness in the air. Somehow the insects have gotten word that summer is ending and are on the march. A steady flotilla of monarchs sails into the yard, riding an invisible tide. Each butterfly sips from the garden flowers as it begins its long trek south to Mexico, where it will wait out winter in dense fir groves on the slopes of volcanic mountains. There it will not be cold enough to freeze the butterflies, yet it will be cool enough that they can survive in a low-energy state akin to hibernation, except for occasional nectar snacking on warm days.

Large green darner dragonflies stitch the sky with their frantic zig-zag flight as they too forsake the Gulf of Maine for the Gulf of Mexico. These frenetic dragonflies can travel nearly one hundred miles a day if they hitch a ride on winds heading south, and they appear to navigate using the lay of the land, often following the shoreline. Like most migrating songbirds, dragonflies have stopovers every few days during which they rest and feed. But some don't survive their journey south, which can stretch more than a thousand miles, and roads are often littered with their carcasses this time of year.

While walking the other day with my neighbor Beth and looking for the first fall leaves, I spot something glinting on the road. As we get closer, I discover it is the iridescent wings of a large dead dragonfly, its body perfectly preserved. After picking it up, I cup it in my hand so I can bring it back to adorn my windowsill with its intricate design. Beth and I continue walking and talking about her upcoming migration down south and all the packing and planning it entails. Beth is a retired schoolteacher and music lover who lives on the peninsula in a large log cabin she and her husband built that has only a woodstove to heat it. With family ties in Pennsylvania and the siren songs of symphony and opera performances pulling her back to Philadelphia, Beth, like the birds and most of us "from away," usually leaves Maine by the beginning of October.

"I always hate to leave," she tells me, and I'm about to agree with her but instead I sputter and squawk with surprise because I feel a fluttering in the hand cupping the dragonfly. After opening it, the insect miraculously zooms away, not dead after all but merely resting on its long journey south. Beth cackles while I collect my composure. For the rest of our walk, nothing else occurs as eventful as a dragonfly's wings beating in the palm of my hand, akin to that dogfish heart from years ago. But later, while reading a book outside, another dragonfly alights on one of the pages, its lacy wings motionless while its rusty body pulsates. Is it too just catching its breath while flying to Mexico?

Why dragonflies migrate is a mystery. Songbirds journey south in fall to feed on insects and berries not available in the frozen north and then return to their Maine haunts to nest and raise their young. But dragonflies end their migration south by mating and dying, with only their offspring making the return journey north after winter.

Most of the songbirds in Maine are also "from away" and my ears are already missing their melodies, especially those of the lyrical warblers, which have left our forests and followed the insects south. Instead I hear the loud *wick-wick-wick* chants of northern flickers who come from Canada to spend winter in our area. I always know fall is soon to follow when the white rumps of these woodpeckers teasingly flash as they take flight when I bike by.

A few weeks ago, black-bellied plovers preening their distinctive black-and-white tuxedo plumages suddenly made a brief appearance on the large flat rock in our bay that is last to be submerged during high tide. Within days these birds were gone from our sights and may not reappear again until next August. The plovers, like most of the shore-birds we see in Maine, begin their migration south in midsummer, arriving from the Arctic to stay a few weeks in our area so they can bulk up for their more rigorous migration across the ocean, with some travel-ing as far south as Chile and Argentina, often flying more than a thou-sand miles without stopping. Researchers were surprised to discover that sandpipers banded in Maine were seen just forty-eight hours later on the top of South America in Suriname and that larger shorebirds can fly nonstop for as long as nine days.

To make these epic journeys, the birds must build up their fat by feeding day and night on crustaceans, snails, clams, mussels, and worms they dislodge from seaweed and mud. They roost just a few hours on either side of high tide. "It's all about the tides," noted Lindsay Tudor, a wildlife biologist with the Maine Department of Inland Fisheries and Wildlife. "If there's exposed mud on shore, they're out there feeding." And for good reason—without the fat reserves needed to reach their winter homes, the migrating birds plummet into the sea.

Seeing dwindling numbers of shorebirds in their bays over the years, many of my neighbors are outraged at the seaweed harvesting that happens in our area. Rockweed is collected to make packing materials, fertilizer, and thickening agents in everything from paints to puddings. But such rockweed removal might be depriving shorebirds of critical food supplies they need before heading south in fall. Blame for the decline in shorebirds can also be put on oil spills and other environ-mental contaminants, dragging for mussels and scallops, and clam and baitworm harvesting, all of which occur in Maine.

But even if we do our part here to maintain their vital habitat, the environmental deprivations shorebirds may experience on their winter-ing grounds is out of our control, as nature knows no borders, especially for these globe-trotters. Who knows what happens to the shorebirds in

Suriname? Yellowlegs are hunted for sport in the Caribbean and Brazil because they fly into the shore slowly, so are easy shots. "They do all that eating and flying, only to get blasted," Tudor said.

Yesterday while looking through binoculars at what I thought were our year-round resident eider ducks, I instead saw a different sort of duck that had a narrow red beak instead of the eider's distinctive broad sloping yellow schnoz, which reaches up nearly the full length of its black head. Some of the heads of these newcomer ducks were emerald green and smooth; others were rust colored with stiff jagged clumps of feathers stretched out behind them like teenagers with spiked hairdos.

Mergansers!

Their abrupt appearance as they make their way to the bay from freshwater lakes and rivers that will freeze over in winter always marks the beginning of autumn here. Although delighted to see the mergansers, it is a bittersweet reunion for me because cooler weather requiring more time indoors will soon follow in their wake.

The hummingbirds are also attuned to the crisp temperatures to come. They are becoming vicious, anxious to bulk up for their fall migration. With flashes of green iridescence and wings that beat so fast they are just a blur, they chase away other hummingbirds trying to drink from the same flowers or bird feeder. One morning, a hummingbird desperate for nectar even poked at the scarlet hibiscus flowers printed on a friend's pajamas while she sat on her deck!

Their aggressiveness at seeking food is not surprising considering the thousands of miles hummingbirds have to fly before reaching Mexico or Panama. Prior to that long flight south, they have to nearly double their weight, especially those that fly nonstop for more than twenty hours straight to cross the five-hundred-mile-wide Gulf of Mexico. If these tiny birds, weighing only about a tenth of an ounce, don't have enough fuel for this flight, they digest their muscles, bones, and other internal organs. (Knowing this, I'll no longer complain about the back-aching, ten-hour drive home to Philadelphia and the lousy food at the pit stops.) Artic terns, which on rare occasions grace Maine's shores with their buzzy cries, have one of the longest migrations, traveling more than twenty thousand miles from Greenland and Iceland where they breed in summer to the Antarctic where they winter.

No one knows why arctic terns and other birds are driven to take such long journeys when they could find food and shelter closer. Some speculate strong bonds to their nesting grounds drive their return to the Artic each year. "To fly nonstop thousands of kilometers over open ocean without taking a bite of food, a swallow of water, or a minute of sleep is a mind-boggling demonstration of the epic importance of home and of the ability and drive to return to it of even tiny birds," biologist Bernd Heinrich noted in his book *The Homing Instinct.*

And how driven these migratory birds are, with a restlessness in fall that even caged birds experience, hopping or flying in the same southerly direction as their wild brethren take at this time of year. My friend Becky has seen this restlessness in the mallard ducklings she hatches and raises each spring, even though they've never seen other ducks before and trail her all summer as if she were their mother. Each fall, Becky brings them to a pond where there are other mallards that pull them like a magnet. "I don't teach them to go in the water and dive. They do that instinctively. They are drawn to other ducks just like children are drawn to other children," Becky told me.

After dropping them off at the pond, Becky checks on her ducks periodically and finds that initially when she calls out to them, they leave the others and swim toward her, quacking. But eventually they stop responding. "It does break my heart a little when they finally fly away; it's kind of like the way you feel when you drop your kids off at college—you want them to be independent, but you know you'll miss them," she added. One time Becky took her ducks to a pond in Acadia National Park, but they weren't ready yet to return to their own flock. When she returned a few hours later to check on them, they were quacking hysterically at the visitor drop-off in the parking lot, while a bunch of Japanese tourists surrounded them, snapping picture after picture.

There's a loud chorus of birds that happens every fall, so high above us that you need special equipment to detect it, I learned at a talk given by an ornithologist at a nearby inn. While we swatted mosquitos in a refurbished barn, Jeffrey Wells told us that each fall thousands of migratory birds are flying over our heads. These birds migrate mostly at night so they can avoid their predators and take advantage of the cooler and less turbulent nighttime atmosphere. He said that if you focus a telescope on the full moon, you can see the silhouettes of their flocks on the move. Wells had a special device that picked up and amplified the sounds of the migrating birds, and he played us recordings of their ceaseless chatter, which happens while we are sleeping.

In bed last night, thinking about all those birds flying over me, I wondered if their chitchat might penetrate my dreams in some way and subconsciously make me restless. Although in Maine for another month, I begin to sense the end of summer and my own upcoming migration south. I start to bulk up on insights that can nourish me when I return to the hustle and bustle of the cementscape, gleanings that will sustain me in the winter months to come.

Spending an entire summer in Maine is transformative. When first arriving each year, it's on the tailwinds (or should I say hot air?) of personal professional ambitions—the frenetic need to be productive, to promote, to essentially shout out, "Look what I can do!" You have to be pushy to succeed in the highly competitive world of freelance writing, which means not only pushing myself to continually produce, but pushing others to pay attention to what I produce.

Although continuing to work on regular writing assignments, once in Maine I don't aggressively pursue additional articles, but instead fill extra time observing and reflecting. After spending a few weeks by the bay, professional pushiness subsides and I begin to pull in what's around me.

The tide starts coming in.

I pull in the loons' cries, the seals' growls, and the flute-like serenades of the wood thrushes at sunset. I pull in the smells of the sweet ferns, pines, and firs and the childhood memories they stir. I pull in the night sky's starry glitter and the infinitude it suggests. With all senses on high alert, pulling everything in expands my horizons such that the trajectory of personal ambition loses force and direction, and problems are diluted by the natural world that engulfs them.

When I was fourteen, my problems dissolved upon seeing the night sky in Maine for the first time. (In prior summers spent up north, I was probably too young to stay up late enough to see this spectacle.) At the time I was a typical teenager besotted with hormones and could barely see past my own nose. Having grown up in the suburbs where endless streetlights obscured the night sky, I always assumed there were only a handful of stars, and these bright lights were cupped in the Big Dipper.

But one clear evening that summer in Maine, I, like most adolescents late at night, couldn't fall asleep. Long after my parents were snoring in their bedroom, I bundled up to protect myself from both mosquitos and the chill in the air and went out on the deck of the cabin at which we were staying. My eyes not adjusted to the enveloping darkness, I inched my way across the deck with hands outstretched to warn of any upcoming obstacles. Finally reaching the deck's railing, I turned around and leaned against it. Looking up, expecting to detect the usual small grouping of stars, not realizing at the time how meager they were, I was astonished to see the sparkling cloud of the Milky Way stretched across the sky—endless stars coalescing into the white filigree of our own galaxy, like a rivulet of spilt milk flowing across the black hemisphere of night above. It was both a humbling and expanding experience. Humbling in the sense of realizing my minute place in space, yet expansive in realizing I was part of something much bigger than myself. Just as there was something freeing in seeing the last ashy remains of my mother become part of the vast ocean, I think it will, in some way, be liberating to one day be stardust again and scattered in the infinite cosmos.

But not everyone feels comfortable with that vastness and the forces of nature that foment continual change. One of my favorite stories about Maine that a writer relates in *The Natural World of Louise Dickinson Rich* is that of her city-slicker friend who comes up to spend a month on the Schoodic Peninsula with the hopes of relieving his health problems. But after only a week, this friend is packing his bags, remarking, "The tide comes in and the tide goes out; and then it comes in and then it goes out, twenty-four hours a day, seven days a week. And that's all there is to it. Nothing else happens, and it doesn't accomplish a thing, and there's nothing you can do about it. It's driving me crazy. I've got to get away from it."

Too bad this gentleman never learned to appreciate the cyclical beauty of the tides, the ocean's rhythmic heartbeat that reassuringly marks time in the short term, while more subtly wearing down rocks to sandy beaches to be strolled on by later generations. He could have tuned in to the ceaseless motion of our planet, which is the opposite of stagnation, and seen the long timelines of change that eventually turn a multitude of cycles into a spiral. It is the spiral that is the key to this world, whether it is embodied in our DNA or our Milky Way galaxy—a cycling spiral that has both symmetry and movement forward. Each generation dies, but not without leaving its imprint, passing something on for the next one to carry forward, as the butterflies, beach cobbles, and my family showed me. My brother and parents have never left me because they are firmly embedded in who I am and how I operate: Joe is there when I am still enough to notice the dragonfly landing on my book; my mother is there when I gaze out at the bay appreciating its natural beauty and undercurrents of meaning; and my father is there when I wonder what causes the wind that ripples the water and carries the arctic terns on their trek to the bottom of the globe. My family has shaped me along with this wild Maine shore, whose contours have determined where I feel most at home.

The steady drumbeat of death has also shaped me, shapes all of us forced to listen, mortality making us more aware that the flip side of death is life. The Buddhists have an exercise in which you meditate while lying inside a coffin, an experience aimed at making you recognize the transient nature of your life. Losing my brother and parents in what my sister-in-law Elke called "the decade of death" has made me savor and experience more fully each moment before it slips away. To be grateful for the opportunity to walk on this earth and be mesmerized by all its ephemeral wonders and mysteries: the thin ribbon of fog suspended in midair; the glittery dance of wind and light on the water; the intricate aerial choreography of a swooping shorebird; the pulsating wings of a gilded dragonfly; the throbbing of a persistent heart. As the Roman philosopher Seneca once wrote, "You must match time's swiftness with your speed in using it, and you must drink quickly as though from a rapid stream that will not always flow."

Time in Maine hasn't solved all of my spiritual dilemmas or quenched my curiosity about the natural world. But I accept that there always will be mystery and more to explore, because the more we know, the more questions we learn to ask, and the deeper we have to dig to find the answers. Becky claims science takes away the mystery, the spiritual sense of things. But I feel quite the opposite. Each scientific fact I learn about a butterfly, migrating birds, or the tides fills me with both amazement at what is known and wonder at what we still need to divine. There is so much more than meets the eye, like skeins of birds high in the sky susurrating, their winged forms silhouetted by the harvest moon while we slumber unaware. The next time I return to Maine, when the fields are spiked with indigo lupines and the woods resonate with the love songs of birds, I'll have new things to discover as well as new spiritual conundrums to solve by sojourning along its tree-lined shore.

The meaning is there. I just have to find it.

Epilogue

She squeals, she squirms, and she waves her arms above her, conducting an orchestra no one can see, all the while bouncing her legs against the high chair and practicing her consonants *ba* and *da* with glee. She's a bundle of energy with a grin for everyone who greets her. We shuffle in for breakfast, silent and somnolent until we drink our morning coffee, slow to warm up to another day, with so many days behind us the same. But not Jo—she is new to this world and everything in the world is new to her—she whips her head in response to the sound of the coffee grinder, bunches up her brightly colored bib, bringing it into her mouth to explore further, and tracks the squirrel outside the window as it bounds across the lawn. She swivels both her body and her attention from one thing to another, not wanting to miss out, her enthusiasm contagious, her energy relentless, her zest for life delightful. If she had words in her mind, there would be nonstop excited chatter: *A bird! Grandma! Flowers! Bacon sizzling! A squirrel! Flowers! Grandma!* She's the granddaughter my brother will never meet, the great-grandchild my parents will never hold, the first of a fresh new generation eager to make the acquaintance of everything.

The healing mascot for our family, Jo answers the ultimate question, *Why is there decline and death followed by birth and life?* That answer surfaces when I see her unblemished by experience, her eyes sparkling with excitement, her body pulsating with life's heartbeat, her entire being ready to explore:

To refresh the wonder.

Acknowledgments

It takes a village to write a decent book and I am grateful to the fellow writers, friends, and family too numerous to mention by name who commented on earlier renditions of the chapters in this book and helped shape it into its current form. Extra thanks are due to Janet Falon, who suggested I compile my essays into a book, and Jonathan Callard for his creative nonfiction writing classes and his detailed critiques. I'm also grateful to Sy Montgomery for being so enthusiastic about my writing, encouraging me to publish, and leading me to Down East Books. There I am thankful for Michael Steere, who recognized my book "was more than just a memoir" and took it under his wing. Thanks are also due to the scientists Duane and Ruth Braun, Bernd Heinrich, Edvard Moser, and Kate Petrie, who reviewed for accuracy various sections relevant to their areas of expertise. I'm also grateful for the friends and family who make appearances in the book and graciously let me write about them, and for my loving and supportive husband Frank Chudnow who jokes that he is not in the book enough. Finally, I am especially grateful to Maine and how it has shaped me and my understanding of the natural world, sustained me through difficult times, and continues to awe me with its beauty.